The Silver, the Gold, and the Glory

The Silver, the Gold, and the Glory

Dr. Christian Harfouche

Power House Publishers
Pensacola, Florida

Unless otherwise indicated, all scriptural quotations are from the
King James Version of the Bible.

The Silver, the Gold, and the Glory
Published by:
Power House Publishers
Christian Harfouche Ministries
4317 N. Palafox St.
Pensacola, FL. 32505
850-439-9750

Editorial Consultant: Phyllis Mackall, Broken Arrow, Oklahoma

Cover design and book production by:
DB & Associates Design & Distribution
dba Double Blessing Productions
P.O. Box 52756, Tulsa, OK 74152
www.dbassoc.org

Printed in the United States of America.

Contents

Foreword

1. The Antidote to Lack 1

2. Power To Get Wealth 27

3. The Hidden Riches of the Last Days 45

4. Revelation Produces Wealth 69

5. Peace and Prosperity Come to the Temple 89

6. Faith, Confession, and the Promises of God 105

7. The Blood Erased the Curse! 131

8. Paid in Full! 157

Foreword

This book on the *Silver, the Gold, and the Glory,* written by my dear friend, Dr. Christian Harfouche, is a prophetic book for these end times, concerning finances.

The church has remained in the "middle ages" concerning finances. But God is wanting to do awesome things through the 21st century Church. Things that have never been done before. We are living in the costliest age of human history. The Gospel is free, but it takes a lot of finances to get the Gospel out.

As you read this book, ask the Lord to open your spiritual eyes and allow God's wisdom to be imparted to you. Jesus said that the children of the world are wiser in the affairs of money than the children of the light (Luke 16:8).

I believe that this book will be a great blessing to you as you read it prayerfully. Christian is a great man of God and I consider it a blessing to have him as my dear friend.

> God's Blessings
> Dr. Rodney M. Howard-Browne
> Tampa, Florida
> June 1999

The Silver, the Gold, and the Glory

Chapter 1

The Antidote to Lack

I am saddened when I see Christians who can't pay their bills.

I am saddened when I see men and women of God who have a vision, yet they have no one to help them plow through to victory in the next dimension in God.

I am saddened when I see "religion" give Christians opinions and traditions rather than the Word of God.

The Spirit of the Lord has laid it on my heart to write this book on *The Silver, the Gold, and the Glory* because there are so many misconceptions about prosperity and God's will to supply the Christian's need.

"Money Cometh!"

In fact, this book has been burning in me so strongly of late that the Spirit of the Lord began to shout in my heart, "Money cometh! Money cometh! Money cometh!"

However, unless we deal with the misconceptions, lies, traditions, and rituals being taught about prosperity, we will never be able to effectively step into the next move of God, which will be *the greatest transference of wealth ever!*

Did you know that as a Christian you can choose *not* to be led by the Word of God? God will not force you to be led by the Word, but He will develop a desire for the Word in you.

1

You must become so strong in God's Word that you can say, "I don't care if no one else believes this. It's written here in the Word, and I know it's the truth."

The silver, the gold, and the glory are mentioned repeatedly throughout the Bible. As a matter of fact, we serve a God of glory.

People talk about praising God, but when you ask them what for, they don't know, because most of their "religion" consists of no absolutes. How can you praise God without any absolutes?

How can you praise God and say He's *good* when in the back of your mind you are not sure He's good, or He might do something you won't understand or like? It doesn't make any sense.

If God has already done something for me or supplied me with things — even if I don't have them and I just *hear* about them — my job is to *believe* it. And if I believe it, I'm going to praise Him for it!

Five Things God Has Already Done for You

The five things God has already done for you that you need to know about contradict religion so badly, most churches would shut down, simply based on Psalm 8 alone.

Verse 3 says, "When I consider thy heavens, the work of thy fingers, the moon and the stars, which thou hast ordained." This is science. When I consider the work of God — the galaxy, the stars, the sun, the moon — and see how awesome creation is, what does it lead me to conclude?

The answer is found in verse 4: "What is man, that thou art mindful of him? and the son of man, that thou visitest him?" This is one thing you can know better than you know your own name: *God is mindful of you.* That means He's got you on His mind!

If you are a parent and you've got your child on your mind, do you plan to abuse that child? Not if you're a good parent, you don't. If you're a good father or mother, what you have in mind for your child are plans for good.

You are thinking of the child now, you are thinking of the child tomorrow, and you will be thinking of the child when he grows up. You have plans for your child. And you can be more sure than anything that God has you on His mind.

Why Christians Worry Needlessly

Here's another good thought: If God has us on His mind, why do most Christians act as if God doesn't have them on His mind, and they have to worry about themselves? They think if they don't worry about themselves, no one else will. Therefore, they run around mindful of themselves when they should be mindful of God.

They consider themselves and the works of their hands, and then they ask God to help them when they need to consider the works of His hands. Why did He make the stars, the moon, the sun, and so forth? He made them because He was mindful of us!

Second, *God visits you.* You can be sure of the fact that God will visit you. God has visited man. Two thousand years ago, He sent His Word and healed them!

A woman in my congregation told me that her young son was visiting his grandmother when she said, "We've got to go get your asthma medicine."

The boy said, "Grandma, I don't have asthma."

She said, "What do you mean? Of course you have asthma."

"No, I don't have asthma."

"Don't argue with me. You've got asthma."

"Grandma, I don't have asthma! I've been healed."

"When were you healed?"

The child answered, "Oh, two thousand years ago I was healed."

I'm sad to say that the majority of the church world doesn't know, let alone believe, that two thousand years ago God sent His Word and healed and delivered them from all their destructions.

Yet a little child knew it.

Visited and Crowned

I've been visited by God. God came down to Earth and did what I could not do so I would believe it and walk in the fullness of it. That's the second thing He did.

The third thing He did for you and me is found in Psalm 8:5, "Thou hast made him a little lower than the angels, and hast crowned him with glory and honour." God is mindful of you; God visited you; and *God crowned you!*

Did you know you're crowned? A beggar isn't crowned. That's why it's called the Gospel, because it's the *good news.* God crowned you with glory and honor. God put a crown on you; He didn't put a straw hat or hood on you. Crowns are placed on kings, and the Bible says God has made us kings and priests unto God (Revelation 1:6).

Unfortunately, most Christians don't resemble or act like kings at all, because they haven't heard the good news. They don't know God is thinking about them. They don't think God visited them, and they certainly don't think they're crowned with anything, much less glory and honor!

What Are You Crowned With?

My Bible says you only give honor to whom honor is due. How did I deserve honor? I didn't, but Jesus paid the price, and because He was crowned, I am also crowned. I am due honor because of Christ.

Do I seek my own honor? No, I seek His honor. Jesus is the King of kings — and believers are born into the kingdom to be kings.

Your *attitude* affects your *latitude*. The world is stealing Christian principles and using them in corporate settings, while the children of God are acting like simpletons who do not know the benefits God has supplied for them.

You must know what you're crowned with. God didn't crown you with depression, so don't hold your head down and walk around as if worldly circumstances and the devil have dominion over you.

Most Christians talk more about the devil than they do about God! But let me tell you something: The devil knows who the kings crowned with glory and honor are. The devil said, "Jesus I know, and Paul I know…" (Acts 19:15).

You Have Dominion

"What is man, that thou art mindful of him?" The psalmist David was considering the heavens, the work of God's fingers, and he concluded that all the glory was created for man.

God crowned man with glory and honor and made him to have dominion over the works of His hand — and He put all things under his feet. So *the fourth thing God did was make you to have dominion.*

People are not mature Christians until they take the dominion they were created to have. God didn't say He made Christians to be *under* the circumstances, and He didn't say He made them to be prisoners of those circumstances. Instead, God made Christians to have dominion over the work of His hands!

The work of God's hands includes the things He put on planet Earth. In the next verse, Psalm 8:6, God says not only did He make you to have dominion, but He also put all things under your feet. This includes the sheep kingdom, the cattle kingdom, the bird kingdom, the fish kingdom, and so forth. They are included in "all things" — *and that translates into money!*

The fisherman sells his catch for money, and the cattleman and the shepherd sell cattle and sheep from their herds for money. God put all these things under man's feet, so He must be mindful of man.

Theologians will tell you that man was created to worship God, but it's not like God didn't have anyone to worship Him. He had the angels, and He really didn't need to create a substitute for them. Some say that man was created to have dominion. Like worship, dominion is included in why man was created, but that's not the real reason, either.

The Purpose for Your Existence

In this chapter, you will discover the ultimate purpose for your existence. You were created for a reason. You have a destiny. Some of the things you do in this earthly life will have an eternal impact. That's our primary message.

Each of you was predesigned by God to make an impact upon this planet. Throughout eternity, people will talk about your accomplishments. Some are going to be in heaven because of you, and others will be in heaven because of them.

What, then, is the ultimate purpose for your existence? Genesis 1:26 reads: "And God said, *Let us make man in our image*, after our likeness: and let them have dominion over the fish of the sea, and over the fowl of the air, and over the cattle, and over all the earth, and over every creeping thing that creepeth upon the earth."

So the ultimate purpose for man's creation is for man to resemble his Creator. How were you created? You were created in His image. Why are you born again? You are born again to be conformed to the image of His dear Son.

God made man, blew into him the breath of life, and man became like God. But when Adam sinned and fell from that state of resembling his Father, he began to resemble the devil. He fell from *the image of God* into *the image of Satan*.

6

Jesus confirmed that when He said to the Pharisees, "Ye are of your father the devil, and the lusts of your father ye will do…" (John 8:44). To think, these were the religious people He was addressing!

When the Last Adam Came

Someone will ask, "God is the Father of us all, so how did the Pharisees end up with the devil as their father, and why does the Bible say that we were bound to Satan and sin before Christ came?

God sent Jesus. Hebrews 1:3 tells us that Jesus is the brightness of God's glory and *the express image of His person.* Jesus was the first man since Adam fell who was the perfected image of God. As a matter of fact, the Bible calls Him "the last Adam" (1 Corinthians 15:45).

Few in the church world believe you are supposed to be like God. Church leaders don't tell you that you were born again to be in God's image so when people run into you, they will literally see God in motion in and through you. They don't tell you that — but that's why Jesus came!

What Adam Lost Through the Fall

Not only did Adam fall from being in the image of God through sin or high treason; he also fell from the dominion God had given him. This means he fell from being like God — *and he fell from his wealth and riches.*

When Adam was cast out of the Garden of Eden, he was cast out from where the fruit was. He was cast out from where the land cooperated. He was cast into a place of thorns and thistles. Cherubim kept him from returning to the garden until the seed of the woman — the Lord Jesus Christ — came to deliver him!

Deliver Adam from what? The three things that happened to him after he fell: (1) *spiritual death,* (2) *sickness and disease,* and (3) *poverty.*

So all of a sudden this man who was created and crowned with glory and honor fell from the image he was created in through the high treason of sin. When he did, he fell from the dominion he had over the things God had created him for.

If that is the case and Jesus came to seek and to save that which was lost, it is good news. *It is good news that you don't have to be sad or broke anymore!*

Jesus said, "It is finished!" That sealed it. God doesn't need to do another thing to redeem or to save that which was lost. Thus, we must conclude that Jesus did every-thing necessary to redeem that which was lost. What was lost? The image of God was lost.

The Image of God on Earth

You couldn't find it on planet Earth until Jesus came, and when He came, people didn't recognize Him, because they weren't accustomed to the image of God. They thought He was a demoniac! They thought He worked by Beelze-bub! They never saw the image of God in Him.

Why? Because no one was walking around talking to storms with authority. What was that? Dominion. They said, "What kind of a man is this?"

Have you ever read Genesis? Jesus was the kind of man God had intended. God had him in mind all along.

The people of Jesus' day weren't accustomed to seeing a man talking to the dead and commanding them to live. That's called dominion. It was missing. Why? The image of God was missing.

The people weren't accustomed to seeing the image of God in motion. When they saw Jesus, they saw someone who ruled over nature, someone who ruled over the laws of lack and poverty, the laws of sickness and disease, and the law of sin and death. They saw someone who was completely and totally free. Although He was *in* the world, He was not *of* the world. When the devil came to tempt Him, Jesus had nothing in him.

The people of Jesus' day saw someone who wouldn't have even died unless He submitted Himself willingly to death by crucifixion. They weren't accustomed to that. They had never seen a man like that.

Sad to say, since the Early Church, we haven't seen too many like Him. And when we see one, we criticize him until he dies, and then we write books about him and say how great he was.

For example, when I read about John G. Lake, the great missionary-statesman to Africa, I wonder why the man wasn't as popular when he was alive. Many authors are writing about him today.

I also wonder why Smith Wigglesworth, the famed English evangelist and apostle of faith, was persecuted by the religious world while he was alive but became a sudden hero overnight after he died.

The Image of God

Why is this? It's because people are so accustomed to *the image of religion*. People are accustomed to the image of humanity. People are accustomed to the image of sympathy. They are *not* accustomed to the *image of God;* and when you begin to put on the image of God, you will have to deal with men's criticism. But be of good cheer: I'd rather have the acceptance of Jesus than the acceptance of man.

Religion teaches you foolishness. It says, "The reason you are suffering is so that you can know how to minister to someone who is suffering." If that is true, should I become an alcoholic so I can minister to alcoholics or a homosexual so I can minister to homosexuals?

Religion tells you, "The reason you're poor is so that you can minister to the poor." I'll tell you who can minister to the poor. It's the generous rich person who can show them the way out of poverty. Two poor people will agree and sympathize with one other all the way to the grave. They need someone with the ability to help them — and ability doesn't always come through experience.

9

Most religion is sympathetic toward human nature and resistant toward the things of God. There has been so much Word preached, most Christians have heard the truth. But some Christians can't get out of the dead ruts they are in, because it demands a decision from them that is not based on sympathy.

Most people want to hear someone who understands them rather than someone who understands God and His ways. Most people want to hear someone who says, "I know what you're going through." When they find someone sympathetic, they think, "Isn't he wonderful? He's a good minister."

Really? That's like getting shot and someone comes along and says, "I was shot once. I know what you're going through" — but then he walks away and leaves you bleeding to death!

The people of Jesus' day weren't accustomed to the image of God. The image of God not only walked in the human realm; it brought divine ability — and people weren't accustomed to that.

Jesus As a Historic Figure

Religion today is still not accustomed to the image of God. Most preachers today open the Book and talk about Jesus as if He were a historic figure.

If you ask them, "Why doesn't Jesus do those things today?" they say, "Oh, He does — when He wants to." That's because to them He is not only historic; He is foreign.

That's like an ambassador from the United States who hasn't been in this country or had any communications with it for 30 years.

What kind of a report can he give? When asked, "What is happening back home?" he has to say, "I don't know. I haven't been there lately."

A minister must not only know that God is not historic; he must know that God is the God of the *now*. He must know God through a life-long relationship.

Kings Get Gifts

Whenever we delve into the silver, the gold, and the glory and talk about prosperity, Christians may try it for a month or a year, but they don't fully understand it.

They do not understand that money is not something you go after. Money is something that runs you down, chases you down, and overtakes you!

Kings don't have fund-raising events. Kings don't go door-to-door asking for help. People bring gifts to them.

When Jesus was born, He received an offering of gold, frankincense, and myrrh — all of which had immense monetary value. Jesus was just born! He was lying in a manger! You ought to get born again. All of a sudden you will get loaded down with precious things.

From the East, wise men followed the work of God's hand. A star led them all the way to this obscure manger; not even to the inn in Bethlehem. God moved the wise men to come and give honor to whom honor was due (Matthew 2:1-12). Notice they came to give an offering to Jesus even though He was just a baby.

Associating With God

There are two things you must know:

First, you are a king and a priest. What does a priest do? A priest is committed to the full-time service of God.

John G. Lake said, "God's purpose in the creation of mankind was to develop an association on His own plane. Otherwise, God would have been eternally living with babies or imbeciles. The reason God created you is to have an association with Him on His own plane" (John G. Lake, *Book of Quotes*, Harrison House, Tulsa, Oklahoma).

I can't have an association with God on His own plane *intellectually* or *physically*. I can only have an association with Him on His own plane *spiritually*, because it is my spirit that has been born again of God and communicates with Him on His level.

Some say, "Oh, you can't communicate with God." Then how could God say, "Come now and let us reason together, saith the Lord"? How can I reason with God unless I reason with Him around His Word?

Jesus came to seek and save that which was lost; to redeem you back to the image from which you fell. If you return to your former image, you will also return to the position of dominion from which you fell.

I'm going to preach this until poverty is run out of the Church! It doesn't belong in the Church; it belongs in the world. If I'm poor, I want it to be because I gave everything I had to the kingdom, not because I don't have enough to pay my bills.

Jesus' Temptations

And the devil, taking him up into an high mountain, shewed unto him all the kingdoms of the world in a moment of time.

And the devil said unto him, All this power will I give thee, and the glory of them: for that is delivered unto me; and to whomsoever I will I give it.

If thou therefore wilt worship me, all shall be thine.

Luke 4:5-7

When I studied the temptations of Christ, I saw something phenomenal: *Jesus was resisting the devil as a man anointed by the Holy Ghost,* because God cannot be tempted! And the Bible was written by the Holy Ghost and cannot lie. The Bible says Jesus was tempted, so He had to be tempted as a man. Also, He had to resist the devil as a man anointed by the Holy Ghost, or else you and I could never be expected to resist the devil.

The Temptation of Food

The first temptation concerned *food,* which is something man needs to exist. "If You are the Son of God, command these stones to be made bread," Satan taunted. Why? Because Jesus was hungry. He had been in the wilderness for 40 days without food, and now He was hungry. So Satan came and said, "Come on now — think of your belly!"

Many people spend their whole lives fearful of going hungry. Go ahead and slave like a beggar without a Redeemer then. You've forgotten the Gospels. Forget that you have a crown. Forget that you have a God who is mindful of you; a God who supplies all your need according to His riches in glory by Christ Jesus (Philippians 4:19).

The devil said, "Command these stones to be made bread." Jesus said, "Man does not live by bread alone" (Luke 4:4). He meant, "Listen, there is a spiritual part of man that he must make a priority."

Was Jesus hungry? Certainly. But He was not about to compromise His purpose, use God's power to feed Himself, and get out of fellowship with God and His Spirit. Later on, an angel appeared to Jesus in the Garden of Gethsemane and strengthened Him (Luke 22:43).

The Temptation of Trust

The next temptation the devil hit Jesus with was, "If You are the Son of God, cast Yourself down from the pinnacle of the Temple. God has given His angels charge over You, to keep You" (Luke 4:9,10). The devil was questioning God's readiness to *protect* His people.

Protection is yours. The devil will draw your attention to someone who didn't get protection and ask you why. You ought to say, "Go ask God. He knows why."

The devil wants to tell you that person who didn't get protection was worthy of it. He wants your faith to be attached to a circumstance or, if that fails, he wants you to get enough human confidence to jump off a cliff just to see if God will protect you! That's why some people say, "I tried faith. It just didn't work."

Why should you jump to see if God is protecting you when He is protecting you while you're standing? Right now He is mindful of you.

The Temptation To Replace God

The third thing the devil tempted Jesus with was all the kingdoms of the world and the glory of them — the wealth, the honor, and the prestige. He said, "If You worship me, I will give You all of this."

He wanted Jesus to fall from the image of God. He wanted Jesus to *turn away from God as His source* and worship him instead.

In order to worship someone, you must be mindful of that person and his or her attributes. I can't worship God unless I know His attributes. But because I know Him, I can say to Him, "I worship You. You are holy. You supply my needs. You take care of me. You provide." Those are God's attributes.

The moment you stop looking to God as your source and start looking to your job, your business, or anything else as your source, you are in trouble. None of these things is supposed to replace God as your priority.

"Selling Out"

People who are new in the faith may start getting results in a certain area and get so wrapped up in their blessings, they put all their time and energy into that area and forget about God. Soon they "sell out," because they become disoriented. Instead of God being their source, that thing becomes their source, and now they've stooped to a natural level.

This temptation of Jesus would have snared any person who was going after fame and fortune — anyone. However, Deuteronomy 28:2 promises that the blessings of the

Lord will follow you and overtake you. God will protect you.

You don't need to jump off the pinnacle of the Temple. God will feed you. You don't need to fend for yourself either spiritually, using spiritual gifts to get these things, or naturally, using human efforts to obtain them.

Some will ask, "Shouldn't I work?" Yes, but the Bible talks about the laborer doing his job as unto the Lord.

All these kingdoms Satan was offering Jesus were going to become His anyway. Adam gave them away, but Jesus was going to take them back. However, He wasn't going to get them back by acknowledging Satan's lordship; He was going to get them back by overthrowing Satan's power! He really *did* spoil principalities and powers and make a show of them openly (Colossians 2:15).

A Lifetime Commitment

In Matthew 22, we find three things you must have in your life for this relationship with God to work, because this is a lifetime commitment.

First, you must live right. You must live for God. God doesn't mind your having hobbies. He doesn't mind your having fun. He doesn't mind your having things at all.

But He *does* mind when you make your hobby or your things your god. He minds when you forget that all these things are extra, and you make them the main interest in your life, and you make Him a secondary someone who is there like Santa Claus to help you.

Some people do that, and then they blame it on the message, the Word of God. The Word of God never condones living for ourselves or our appetites. That borders on being a heathen!

Another thing to beware of is getting a private revelation on prayer, prosperity, or some other area. Soon you will get totally caught up in prayer or prosperity to the exclusion of everything else, including your relationship with God.

The Spirit of the Lord will warn you all along, saying, "Get back in balance. Don't do that. Don't let the thief steal what I gave you." It doesn't make the prosperity message any less effective, but it's an extra emphasis. Real prosperity is having the image of God on the inside of you.

If you don't yield to the Spirit, wanting to take control of yourself, you will get shipwrecked. That's why it's so important to live right. If you don't, you'll open your life up to the attack of the enemy.

Why? Because your shield of faith won't work. When you walk in condemnation, your heart condemns you. Your petitions are not heard by God, and you can't be protected.

How do you know when you're starting to get away from God? Here's a good way to know if you're living right. You can get caught up in ministry. But the next thing you know, instead of tithing, you keep the money, because you're a minister. The easiest thing to do — the first step toward going broke — is to tithe to yourself.

You've got to understand you can't appear before God and give Him what hasn't cost you anything. The moment you do that, it gets easier the second time, and then the next time. Soon, your heart is far from God.

Why? Because your wallet is where your treasure or heart is. And when you compromise the way you give, you'll compromise the way you live.

Think Right

The second thing you must do is think right. You can't think wrong and live right. Temptation starts in the thought life. You may wonder what is wrong with going after what God told you to do and putting all your energy and efforts into it. What is wrong with it is, if God told you to do it, He didn't tell you to make it your god!

For example, God could speak to you about your future husband or wife and say, "That's the person you're going to marry."

If you're not careful, you'll take that word and run with it. You'll spend no time with God, no time in the church, or no time in ministry. Everything about you will become so focussed on that person, he or she will be substituted for God in your life.

Then, when you mess the whole thing up, you'll think, "Maybe I didn't hear God." Yes, you heard God, but He never said this person was going to be your *god;* He just said he or she was going to be your *mate!*

If God tells me to do something, He is not telling me to do it because He can't do it. He is just saying, "Son, I am going to supply the ability." But this is what people do: They say, "All right, God. Thank You. I'll take it from here. That's all I wanted to know. Thank You very much."

They want to fit everything into a little "box." Then they run around frantically. Down the line when they don't get any results, they wonder what happened. They stifled the Holy Ghost and then took over themselves — that's what happened!

Talk Right

Third, you must talk right. You must watch your mouth. You cannot step into the blessings of God in any area unless you talk right.

You've got the image of God inside of you, and it is going to grow by the Word of God. And when it does, it's going to be like Christ. It's going to have dominion. It's going to have power in the Earth realm.

I believe with all my heart that there is going to be a great transference of wealth, but it's not going to come because we've worn ourselves out trying to get money. We shouldn't want money; we should want God. Everything else will then be added unto us.

Matthew 22:15 describes a different temptation of Jesus. "Then went the Pharisees, and took counsel how they might entangle him in his talk." Do you know you can get entangled in talk?

Religion and the devil want to entangle you in talk. The way to entangle you is to get you to think wrong; to fight error in your life rather than correct it. In fact, you will get in that mode for extended periods if you allow yourself to.

When You Lack Excitement

You can know you are justifying error when you have absolutely no excitement about doing anything you're hearing. You think, "I've heard that before." Instead, you must tell yourself, "Shape up!"

Verses 16 and 17 say, "And they sent out unto him their disciples with the Herodians, saying, Master, we know that thou art true, and teachest the way of God in truth, neither carest thou for any man: for thou regardest not the person of men. Tell us therefore, What thinkest thou? Is it lawful to give tribute unto Caesar, or not?"

What these men said was flattering, but it was also the absolute truth. "We know You're true," they said. "You teach the way of God in truth. And you don't care for any man, for you regard not the person of men." In other words, "You're not a respecter of persons." That's the image of God. Jesus is the image of God!

If I want the image of God to live in me, I must be true. I must teach the Word of God in truth. And I must stop yielding to anything that will make me a respecter of persons, because the person I get more attached to than God will be the person who pulls me down and causes me to miss it.

The one opinion I respect more than I do my commitment to God will be the opinion that pulls me down. And if I'm living there, it means I'm living in the image of the first Adam. I need to get out of that image and get into the image of God, allowing the image of God to flow and operate in and through me.

Attached to Finances

This is what the Pharisees asked Jesus: "Tell us, what do You think? Is it lawful to give tribute unto Caesar, or not?" (verse 17). This was the representative Church in those days asking Christ, "Should we pay taxes to Caesar?"

The reason they asked Him that was because they loved money, and they wanted to justify robbing Caesar!

They thought, "We're God's people. God gave us a covenant. The Romans shouldn't rule over us. Caesar is not our God." So they asked, "Is it required under the Law for us to pay Caesar taxes?"

The moment we begin to get attached to finances is the moment we begin to lose what we have. *The devil cannot steal anything you put in the hands of God,* including your Christian walk. That means the enemy must first get you to take your problems out of God's hands and put them in your own hands.

The devil will tell you, "You've got to do your best, so take that problem you are concerned about out of God's hands and put it in your own." And guess what happens if you do that? You fall flat on your face, because you simply don't have the ability to solve your own problems!

"Why Tempt Ye Me?"

But Jesus perceived their wickedness, and said, Why tempt ye me, you hypocrites?

Shew me the tribute money. And they brought unto him a penny.

And he saith unto them, Whose is this image and superscription?

They say unto him, Caesar's. Then saith he unto them, Render therefore unto Caesar the things which are Caesar's; and unto God the things that are God's.

19

When they had heard these words, they marvelled, and left him, and went their way.

Matthew 22:18-22

Avenues of Provision

This is awesome, because many of these people were working, and they got paid for their labor. Provision can come in the form of *money* to buy things with, or it can come in the form of *things*.

Some of these people were fishermen. They sold the fish in the market for money. Others sold sheep, turtledoves, or cattle and got money. Now they've got to give Caesar some of their hard-earned money, which they are attached to.

"How can we get away with keeping more of this?" they wondered. So they wanted to trap Jesus.

Not only were they covetous; they were angry at this preacher who was preaching, "God will take care of you. Don't be like the heathen, seeking all these things. Just seek the kingdom, and all these things will be added to you."

They were angry at this preacher who was teaching out in the fields, because people were heaping gifts into His ministry, and He was freely giving to the poor. They were angry because He didn't worry about anything. He didn't even care where He stayed. God opened up places for Him to stay.

They couldn't handle this man who taught the people of God these things — but He was not leading them in a military or political revolution like they expected Him to.

Instead, He told them, "No, don't fight the world's system that way. Get involved in the things of the kingdom of God, and make God your source."

Motivated by Greed

They wanted to trap Jesus, and the motivation of their hearts was greed. So they went to Him and asked, "Is this according to the Law? Is this right?"

He said, "You hypocrites, show me a penny. Whose image is on this money? Whose writing is on it?" "Caesar's," they admitted. He said, "Then it must be Caesar's money, because whatever carries his superscription and image belongs to him."

Their *hearts* should have had an image and a superscription on them, because their hearts once belonged to the Lord. But somehow their hearts no longer belonged to the Lord; they belonged to the penny! They were trying to hold on to the penny with Caesar's image on it.

But Jesus taught, "No, if Caesar's image is on it, it belongs to Caesar. So give to Caesar what is Caesar's, and give to God what is God's."

Do you know your heart is God's? It belongs to Him. It should be full of His image. It should be full of His nature. It should be full of the knowledge of Him. That's who your heart belongs to.

Therefore, the things that are added to you are only *things,* not belongings you become a servant to. The moment you make them your treasure, you shift your heart allegiance from God to things, and you're on your way to running out of resources.

What happens is, your treasures become your treasure. Thieves break through and steal, and moths corrupt. Jesus taught that you should lay up for yourselves treasures *where?* In heaven, where no thief can break through. Why? Because where your treasure is, there will your heart be also. Give to God what is God's.

What Belongs to God?

What belongs to God? My heart. My thought life. *Me.* God put His image in me. Do you know why? Because He put His claim on me. He sealed me. His law is in my heart. It's in my mind. It's in my mouth. It's in my life. I belong to God.

If I belong to God, He will supply everything I need.
Things will never own me. I will own them through God.
Whatever He tells me to do with them, I will be able to do.
And when I operate like that, I will never ever run out of
resources! Miracles in the financial arena, miracles in the
monetary realm, and supernatural breakthroughs are going
to happen in the lives of faithful people. They are going to
come to pass — guaranteed. Why? *So the covenant can be
established.*

Give to God what belongs to Him. Give to God everything about yourself, and keep it in His hands. Don't say,
"I've done that once." Make it a part of your life by doing
it on a daily basis.

If you get a little too attached to something, say, "I'm
going to back off that object and get back into the things of
God." That's a safeguard against getting into error. Not only
that; it's a safeguard against failure. It guarantees happiness!

Worshipping Things

In Luke 4:7, Satan showed Jesus a vision of the kingdoms and said, "If thou therefore wilt worship me, all shall
be thine."

The Bible calls Satan "the god of this world." If he is
the god of this world, then sometimes he will show you an
opportunity, tempting you, "Just put this first in your life,
and you will own it all." Isn't that terrible?

God doesn't mind your *having* things, but He minds
your *worshipping* things. Do you know what the devil steals?
He steals the things you started worshipping. He steals
the things that already have your heart.

Christians tell you, "God took it to get you back to
Him." No, He didn't. The devil stole it because he got you
to worship it. If you had kept it where it belonged — in
the hands of God — the devil couldn't have stolen it!

The Beginning of Miracles

And the third day there was a marriage in Cana of Galilee; and the mother of Jesus was there:

And both Jesus was called, and his disciples, to the marriage.

And when they wanted wine, the mother of Jesus saith unto him, They have no wine.

Jesus saith unto her, Woman, what have I to do with thee? mine hour is not yet come.

His mother saith unto the servants, Whatsoever he saith unto you, do it.

John 2:1-5

Verse 11 tells us that this was the beginning of miracles. It was the first miracle Jesus did. It marked the beginning of His ministry, because it took place in the first week of His ministry.

Verse 1 says it occurred on "the third day." This was the third day after Jesus returned from Jordan with the power of the Spirit on His life. This miracle was what was going to get Jesus' fame spread throughout the region.

Mary's Role in the Miracle

We don't know how many disciples Jesus had gathered so far, but He and His disciples were invited to this wedding. His mother probably picked up by the Spirit of God the making of a miracle. You know how you sometimes pick up something in the Spirit? But then you've got to know how to work with it.

It's not that they had *no* wine; they ran out of the wine they had. Jesus' mother said, "They have no wine." Some of us get so anxious the moment there is a need.

Jesus answered His mother in an interesting way. He wasn't disrespectful toward her. He said, "Madame, what have I to do with you? My hour is not yet come." In other words, He was not going to be led by her natural plea; He was going to be led by the Spirit.

23

You can know what God wants to do and jump ahead and stop it. We must understand it is not by might nor by power; it is by the Spirit of the Lord.

Anxiety never produces supernatural results. Sometimes you will know what God wants to do, but out of fear you get involved and short-circuit the anointing!

Jesus' mother recognized the making of a miracle, so she said, "They ran out of wine. Do something." He replied, "My time is not yet here." She merely told the servants, *"Do whatever He tells you to do."*

How To Face Times of Lack

When you run out of things, it's called "lack." When this happens, people say, "What do you want me to do? It's all gone. I ran out. I don't have any." Here's what you do when you don't have any: *You do whatever Jesus tells you to do!*

As long as you live on Earth, you will experience times of lack. But if you've got Jesus in the party, Jesus in the marriage, or Jesus in the house, *you have the antidote to lack.*

Jesus is in the house. He's right there. Whatever He tells you to do, do it, because the same Jesus who was present at the marriage supper in Cana is living today in your life!

Jesus told the servants, "Fill the waterpots with water." It doesn't say that they asked why. Most people want to work in the ministry and be on staff, but they want to know the *whys* and the *hows* of everything. They complain about their pastor, "Why doesn't he tell us what's happening around here?"

You can't cooperate with a miracle if you reason it away.

It took work to fill those six large waterpots with 162 gallons of water. Yet the servants did it without asking a question. Are you willing to have that kind of a miracle?

Praying Versus Doing

What we usually do is yell, "Help!" Then we pray and want something to materialize. But do you realize there is not one prayer recorded in this account? Most people spend their time *praying* when all they need to do is what Jesus tells them to do. Whatever He tells you to do, *do it!*

Most people are praying while their opportunity passes them by. They're anointed to act, but they simply don't. In the Name of Jesus, go out and live what I am telling you to live! Increase in everything you do. Let it be added to you left and right, and prosper in it.

> Jesus saith unto them, Fill the waterpots with water. And they filled them up to the brim.
>
> And he saith unto them, Draw out now, and bear unto the governor of the feast. And they bare it.
>
> When the ruler of the feast had tasted the water that was made wine, and knew not whence it was: (but the servants which drew the water knew;) the governor of the feast called the bridegroom.
>
> And saith unto him, Every man at the beginning doth set forth good wine; and when men have well drunk, then that which is worse; but thou hast kept the good wine until now.
>
> This beginning of miracle did Jesus in Cana of Galilee, and manifested forth his glory; and his disciples believed on him.
>
> **John 2:7-11**

A Creative Act

The governor of the feast didn't know they were drinking wine made of water. He even praised the bridegroom for keeping the best wine until the end of the feast. But when those servants obeyed Jesus, filling the waterpots with water and then started pouring, that natural water was changed into wine!

Do you know how much 162 gallons of good wine cost in those days? This was a creative miracle that took one substance and brought it up a little higher in value, and the Bible called it manifesting Christ's glory.

It wasn't even something that happened after the resurrection. After the resurrection, Christ entered into His glory. That is why His Spirit is among us today to work.

Do you think He will bless? Do you think if He directs you to do something and you do it, it's liable to turn out good and awesome?

Preparing for the Transference of Wealth

We are in the time when a supernatural, global, financial miracle is in the making. The transference of global wicked wealth is in process while we are studying and preparing for it.

Major breakthroughs of the Spirit are coming your way — but you've got to live right, think right, and talk right to partake of them!

Chapter 2
Power To Get Wealth

Christ's miracle of turning the water into wine and supplying the need of the guests at the wedding at Cana was *a miracle of provision.*

I personally believe that the best wine in those days was non-alcoholic, because it was so difficult to keep wine from fermenting. Sophisticated equipment was needed during those days to keep wine from fermenting. Therefore, fermented wine was the cheaper wine, and non-fermented wine was more expensive, because it had gone through a process of being sealed in such a way that it would not ferment.

The wine Jesus made was non-alcoholic. When Jesus took that water and turned it into 162 gallons of wine, it was an outstanding performance of provision.

If you remember, Jesus had preached in Luke 4:18, "The Spirit of the Lord is upon me, because he hath anointed me to preach the gospel to *the poor...*." Notice, He is anointed to preach good news to the poor. Why? Because the anointing of the Lord is going to work for the poor, to bless them, supply for them, and take care of them.

So the first miracle Jesus did was a miracle of provision. Of course, He provided later on for others when He multiplied the loaves and fishes. But whether you multiply loaves and fishes and supply the need for a lunch or transform water into wine and provide the need for a wedding feast, it's still the same principle. The anointing works to provide a monetary benefit.

Substance Transformed

Jesus manifested His glory through this miracle. Notice, when His glory manifested, *there was a transformation in the very nature of a substance.*

You can go through the Bible and find many times God performed a miracle that literally changed or multiplied a substance or provided one. If He did it then, He can do the same today!

We are living in a time when provision is more important than ever. There has never been a time when so many ministries were involved in missions, evangelism, and other preaching as today. The need for provision is even greater today than it was in the days of Jesus.

Power To Get Wealth

Now let's look at an interesting verse in Deuteronomy 8:18: "But thou shalt remember the Lord thy God: for *it is he that giveth thee power to get wealth,* that he may establish his covenant which he sware unto thy fathers, as it is this day."

God doesn't give you wealth; He gives you *power to get wealth.* Notice why the wealth is given: "That he may establish his covenant...."

"Wait a minute, God! You're giving me power to get wealth so You can establish your covenant?" That's what the Bible says.

"But that's ridiculous. God can establish His covenant with or without me." Yes, He can, but if He does't use you, He will use someone else. Someone is going to realize through the Word of God that He has already given them power as a child of God to get the wealth.

Acquiring Wealth

We learned earlier that you don't acquire wealth when you go after it, because those who receive the provision of

God are not running after the provision; instead, they are seeking the kingdom.

So why are these people in Deuteronomy getting power to get wealth if they're not going after wealth? The motivation must be in establishing His covenant.

They say, "Do you know what? I'm going to succeed. Success is out there for me, because I've got a role to play in establishing God's covenant. Money is going to come my way."

If they are asked, "Is God always going to pay your bills?" they reply, "Yes. How else is He going to use me to establish His covenant? He's not only going to pay the bills; He's going to give me above and beyond, because He knows I'm going to put that money in the kingdom or in the covenant, offering to help establish His covenant."

That is their confidence. They know they have the power to get wealth. The power to get it is the focus, the desire, or the burning fire in them to establish the covenant.

Have you ever had a desire to be used by God? If you have, sometimes your mind will say, "Who do you think you are to be used like that?"

You didn't invent that desire. God put that desire there. And if God put it there, He will give you the ability to fulfill it.

We must understand that the Bible itself talks about the ability to acquire wealth to establish His covenant.

"Rich" Is Relative

Here is where most Christians miss it. They think, "Wealth...that means when I'm rich, I'll be able to establish the covenant." But that's not what God said, and the reason is because the term "rich" is relative.

For example, who is rich? Someone will say, "Rich is having $1 million." But that's not really rich to a person who has $1 billion. And $1 billion is not really rich to one who has $30 billion.

Do you know why the one who has $1 million is holding onto his million? He thinks he's not rich. He's waiting to get rich. He thinks, "I only have $1 million. I can't spread out. I'll run out of money." And the person who has $1 billion thinks, "I only have $1 billion. I'm not rich. Rich is having $30 billion."

So the word "rich" is relative, and when a child of God traps himself into waiting to acquire enough wealth before he contributes to the work of the kingdom, he is missing out and stepping out of the power to get wealth!

The power to acquire wealth is not something that happens, and then you've got it. The power to get it is something that accompanies you every day of your life as you go about establishing the covenant.

When Wealth Isn't Money

I can take you to places in the world where you're considered rich if you've got shoes! Or if you're a Christian with a nice little house with a table, a few wooden chairs, food on the table, and some clothing, everyone in your church thinks you're rich.

If you are like this person and sow one of your suits in the offering to establish God's kingdom, you open your life to acquire more wealth.

When people say "wealth" today, we automatically assume they've got *money*, but there was a day when wealth didn't mean money. "Wealth" meant that a person was rich in gold, silver, livestock, or other possessions. For example, Abraham was rich in possessions; he owned 300 head of sheep!

So when God said a person has the power to get wealth, He was talking about getting *whatever is necessary* to establish the covenant.

When You Don't Need Money

Today if God tells some people, "I want you to shake such-and-such nation for Me," they wonder, "Where am I going to get the money?"

As a matter of fact, I found out that sometimes you don't need money. If someone sows into your life by giving you a suit, you didn't need money for it. The Bible says God gives us the power to get wealth, but don't lock yourself into a dollar sign.

Don't think, "How am I going to get the money? I only make so much a week. Where is the money going to come from?" Your problem is, you look at your paycheck and ignore the abundance of wealth on planet Earth that God has promised to convert to you from the Gentiles.

You might need to build something, and the building materials could be given to you. You might say, "I don't have anything to give in the offering," but if someone gives you something the ministry needs, you can bring it to the ministry. What have you done? You have exercised the power to get wealth to establish His covenant. You must understand that wealth is not necessarily having a lot of money!

All Things

We found out earlier that God did these five things for man: (1) He is mindful of man; (2) He visited man; (3) He crowned man with glory and honor; (4) He made man to have dominion; (5) and He put all things under man's feet.

When He mentioned "all things," He mentioned the animal kingdom: cattle, sheep, fish, and fowl. That's steak, lamb chops, chicken, and fish!

It is God that gives you the power to get wealth. According to the dictionary, "wealth" mean all property, possessions, and monetary value. The clothes we wear and even the glasses we wear would be considered wealth in some places on Earth.

Someone will say, "I don't consider that wealth." Neither does the man worth $1 million when he's standing next to the man worth $30 million. But *all possessions are wealth.*

Give, And It Shall Be Given Unto You

Nothing is greater than when you're a child of God and things are given to you. The Bible says, "Give, and it shall be given unto you; good measure, pressed down, shaken together, and running over, shall men give into your bosom..." (Luke 6:38).

Often we drop *X* amount of money in the offering and then wait for *X* amount of money to return to get the clue that it multiplied. However, God can return it to you in the form of favors or gifts rather than money.

Someone will argue, "No, every seed produces after its own kind." But if a piece of land is given to me, it is wealth, whether or not I convert it to the same seed, more land. So the word "wealth" means property, possessing something of monetary value, or an abundance of anything.

We want to be like the man who built bigger and bigger barns and said, "I've got a lot of goods stored for many years. Now I can take my ease." That's ridiculous! It's not a description of wealth; it's a description of kicking the bucket, because God said to him, "You fool. Today your soul will be required of you."

Rich in Faith

"I don't have much in the refrigerator." Did you look in the *closet?* The Bible talks about the poor of this world being *rich in faith.*

When was the last time you said, "I don't have anything in the natural, but I'm rich in faith, and faith is the substance of things hoped for. I've got an overabundance of faith!"

The words "rich" and "wealth" in the dictionary mean an abundance of anything. God says you're rich in faith. That means you've got wealth — you're wealthy in faith.

If you were to invite people from a third World country to your home, cook dinner for them, and let them stay in your guest room overnight, they would sware you're rich. And if you told them you're not rich, they would say, "What do you mean? Do you have a car?" "Yes."

"How many shoes do you have?" "I've got a lot of shoes."

Establishing the Kingdom

How many remember that all those shoes in your closet are to establish the kingdom? Come on — every bit of clothing you own is to establish the kingdom.

When my wife and I went into the ministry fulltime, we went into it without a penny. Other than buying groceries, every penny I got I used for the ministry. I either used it to print brochures or to buy ministry clothes so when I appeared in public, I would look like an ambassador of the Lord.

I owned few casual clothes, but I looked like a million dollars when I got in the pulpit! That was to establish the covenant.

If God so chooses, He can make diamonds from coal or turn water into wine. What's the difference if God intensifies the heat and pressure and turns that little bit of carbon into a diamond?

"Oh, you're way out now."

No, we're talking about manifesting God's glory. He said that in the last days, the knowledge of His glory will cover the Earth as the waters cover the sea. But God is not going to go out of His way to perform that in the lives of those who are not establishing the kingdom with what He is pouring into their lives right now.

Releasing the Spirit of Giving

The Spirit of the Lord has been dealing with me on releasing a spirit of giving. Someone will ask, "How could you release the spirit of giving? Only God can do that."

But God has been releasing the spirit of giving for at least two thousand years. He gave heaven's best two thousand years ago when He sent His only begotten Son to die for us!

The spirit of giving that God released must move someone to become an example so someone else can be moved. I want to challenge you that if you see someone in need, do what you can.

"How can I?" some will ask. "I don't have money." You're still stuck on the money issue. Most people would rather have the money to go buy a meal than be given a meal. Why? They feel secure when they've got money in their hand, and that's a problem.

Precious Things

You can be rich in pearls. Where do pearls come from? Sand. Sand goes into an oyster and forms a pearl, and some become pearls of great price. Heaven's gates are made of pearls. I'd like to see those oysters!

Has the devil been doing something in your life to try to irritate you? If you stand on the Word of God, before God is through with you, you'll have something in your hand that is precious, represents wealth, and can be used to establish God's covenant.

You can be rich in diamonds. Did you know a diamond is a mineral of great hardness and refracted power, consisting of carbon, and crystallized under great pressure and temperature?

You can be rich in rubies and sapphires. If so, you could translate those gems into money. Rubies are a kind of aluminum oxide called corundum.

God put all these minerals in the Earth, and men use them. In 1866, a child in South Africa picked up a little pebble that was later identified as a 21-karat diamond. That's what opened up that whole region for diamond mining.

There is a world system that keeps the Church out of its benefits. For example, if all the diamonds in the world were put on the market at the same time, diamonds wouldn't be worth a thing. That's why some are held out.

People don't realize it, but when you begin to teach like this, they think you're materialistic. But all those things are in the Earth to establish the covenant!

The Silver And Gold Are God's

When you find gold in its natural state, it's really gold and silver associated together in one alloy called electrum. "What's that got to do with the Bible?"

It's got a lot to do with the Bible, considering that fact that God said, "The silver is mine, the gold is mine, and I will fill this house with glory, saith the Lord of hosts." God is so smart, He knew that both the silver and the gold were part of the same alloy before we found out about it.

Did you know that there are more than nine billion metric tons of gold in sea water? Even though man was smart enough to discover gold in sea water, no one knows how to extract it efficiently or inexpensively.

Nine billion metric tons translates into more than 19 trillion pounds of gold. How much is an ounce of gold worth — $400? How many ounces are in a pound? And there are more than 19 trillion pounds of gold in the sea.

This is awesome! Almost 20 trillion pounds of gold! That's wealth that cannot be calculated. My calculator doesn't even go that high.

It's in there. Why would God put that much gold in the sea unless maybe He is planning to give someone the idea of how to get it out at the least cost?

Cooperating With God's Plan

If the Bible says God gives you the power to get wealth to establish the covenant, how is this going to happen? Obviously, when you cooperate with God's plan, and your primary desire is to see the kingdom of God and His covenant established and souls saved, *all of these things are added unto you.*

How? In many different ways. People give things to you. Blessings overtake you. And things can also be added to you if you get a divine idea that literally explodes within you.

Gold in the sea is just one example of the untapped wealth that is on planet Earth. However, as of yet, that gold can't be tapped, because no one has had an inspired idea of how to extract it.

Don't tell me God just "happened" to put more than 19 trillion pounds of gold in the sea by mistake, not intending for someone to use this bounty.

Proverbs 10:22 says, "The blessing of the Lord, it maketh rich, and he addeth no sorrow with it." It makes what? *Rich.* This means the blessing of the Lord must be the power to get wealth.

You don't get blessed when you get the wealth; you get blessed when you get the *power* to get the wealth. Even if you have the blessing of the Lord, you may not be rich yet — but the blessing of the Lord does make rich.

Children of God who are walking right will be blessed even when they don't have riches; they will be blessed while they're getting riches; and they will be blessed after they've gotten riches, because their hearts are after God and not after the riches. It doesn't matter where these people are in life; they're rich.

Everything You Need

The devil can't take your faith from you. He can't take your joy. He can't take your contentment. The Bible says, "...godliness with contentment is great gain" (1 Timothy 6:6). Thus, it doesn't matter where you are in life; you've got everything you need in God — and His blessing is sure to make you rich!

When I first got the call of God on my life to go into the ministry, I really didn't have much money, but I became rich in books, tapes, and videotapes. Much of what I know came from that teaching material.

While I was reading and watching, the Spirit was able to bring His own revelations into my heart, even if the speaker wasn't talking about those subjects. Those revelations became wealth to me. I needed teaching materials in those days; I didn't need money.

As we read, Proverbs 10:22 says, "The blessing of the Lord, it maketh rich, and he addeth no sorrow with it." That ties in with First Timothy 6:17: "Charge them that are rich in this world, that they be not highminded, nor trust in uncertain riches, but in the living God, who giveth us richly all things to enjoy."

Notice the phrase "charge them." The word "charge" means "urge" in one translation. It means "command" in another. This letter was written by Paul to Timothy, who was the bishop of the church. He told Timothy to literally *command* the people in that church not to be proud and not to trust in their riches and possessions, but to trust in the living God, who gives us all things richly to enjoy.

Then, in verse 18, he tells them they should do good and be rich in good works, being ready to distribute and willing to communicate.

When the Anointing Is Lost

Now let me ask you this: When did preachers lose this ability to command, charge, or urge those who have possessions how to deal with their possessions and how to live their Christian lives? The answer is: When they lost the anointing!

When you lose the anointing, you lose the blessing God gives that causes you to literally become a magnet that draws the resources necessary for your ministry to exist.

Now you're no longer operating in the blessing; you're operating in the natural. You stop telling people the truth, because you're no longer dependent on God's help. You're dependent on their money, so you stop commanding, rebuking, urging, or correcting them.

As a result, the rich in the church, instead of repenting, become controlling, manipulating, and domineering, and they start jockeying for position. Then, trusting in uncertain riches, they mess up their own lives.

Before long, the devil steals whatever they are trusting in, they end up in lack, the church ends up in lack, and the preacher ends up in lack!

So Paul writes to Timothy and tells him, "I want you to command the rich who are there not to trust in uncertain riches, but to trust in the living God, who gives us richly all things to enjoy."

More and More

If something is given to you *richly*, you're rich in it. For example, most of us are definitely not poor in food. The next time you call yourself "poor," look in the mirror, because "poor" is relative. The next time you get in your car, say, "I'm rich in transportation."

God gives us things richly to enjoy, but not to trust in them or make them our source. Some people hold on to what they own because they think it's not enough. They want more and more. Before long, they're rich in their possessions and trusting in them. But wealth is uncertain, and the devil steals it, because the wealthy missed the whole principle.

When some people first hear the message of faith, they get excited and say, "Do you mean God wants me to have things, and He wants me to be blessed?" Then they change their efforts from establishing the kingdom to getting things.

They say, "Don't you understand? I've got to get these things. It's for the Lord. It's for the kingdom. It's for the covenant." But the Bible never said you must chase riches down.

Instead, the Bible says, "But seek ye first the kingdom of God, and his righteousness; and all these things shall be added unto you" (Matthew 6:33). The devil uses things as a distraction to get believers to go after them in their own ability. If you do go after things in your own ability, you won't succeed.

Rich in Marriage

You could be rich in your marriage. If you marry the right person, you're rich. If you marry the wrong person, you're dead! Having noted that, here's what else the devil does.

Single people say, "How am I going to find a mate in this church? There's no one here I like." So they go to other churches, searching for a mate.

The same principle holds true with finances. People complain, "How am I going to be rich if all I get is a check from my job? It's a dead-end job. Nothing is ever going to happen to me unless I go out and make it happen." They get in the natural, because they don't understand that true riches do not come from a bigger check or more money.

Riches are whatever you need to get the mission or the job done.

God is responsible to bring those things into your life. He gives us richly all things to enjoy.

Great Gain

What does it mean to be rich and have no sorrow attached to your riches? Let's find out about it in First Timothy 6:6-8:

But godliness with contentment is great gain.

For we brought nothing into this world, and it is certain we can carry nothing out.

And having food and raiment let us be therewith content.

Paul wasn't discussing humility in this epistle; he was discussing contentment. They are two different things, because you can have riches and be humble. Otherwise, he wouldn't tell the rich not to be highminded.

Notice where contentment begins. The lowest level of contentment a Christian should settle for is having food and clothing. Actually, in this passage God puts all the necessities of life in a nutshell.

Paul said, "Once you know that God has already committed Himself to the necessities of your life, do not feel inferior because you don't have an overabundance. Otherwise, you will go after gain. If you have food and clothing, the blessings of the Lord make you rich, but you can be content where you are.

Impatient for Riches

Some Christians hear the message of prosperity and give to the kingdom, but they may get to the point where they haven't seen the overabundant return yet. They haven't kept their eyes on the little miracles that God has been doing all along the way.

When they get to that fork in the road, they say, "If God wants me to have that, I'm going to get it!" They start spending money, effort, and resources trying to get the things God has already promised to funnel through them.

Verses 9 and 10 go on to say:

But they that will be rich fall into temptation and a snare, and into many foolish and hurtful lusts, which drown men in destruction and perdition.

For the love of money is the root of all evil: which while some coveted after, they have erred from the faith, and pierced themselves through with many sorrows.

Why did these Christians end up with the kind of riches that have sorrow attached to them when the Word of God promises riches *without* sorrow?

The Love of Money

The key to their problem is found in the phrase, "But they that will be rich...." The key was their priority. They wanted to be rich, so they went after riches.

How do we know that? Because Paul told us *why* they went after riches: for the love of money. They loved money, and they went after it. But if you love God and go after Him, the blessings of God will make you rich, period.

Most people work a lot harder than I do and aren't doing a tenth as well as I am. I work hard, but I'm not working for myself; I'm working hard for the people of God — and I enjoy doing it. It makes a person rich.

Someone will ask, "Are you rich?" It all depends on what you consider rich. If "rich" to you is someone who has $1 million in the bank, no. But that's not the best definition of "rich." If you've got $1 million but you're not giving, you're a poverty-stricken person!

When God's blessing is on you, you can be sure that blessing will take care of all your needs, and God will enable you above and beyond your needs to be able to establish His covenant.

Why? He gave you the supernatural power of the blessing to get the wealth or the abundance of whatever it is you need to establish His covenant with no sorrow attached.

You don't have to chase wealth down; it's chasing you down. But if you won't praise God for what you already have, you can't concentrate on what you don't have. You've got to praise God for what you already have.

Acknowledge Your Blessings

Jesus' disciples told Him, "The multitudes are fainting with hunger. We don't have enough money to go buy bread for them." Money...you've got to have *money* to buy bread.

A little boy in the crowd had a lunch, and he offered it to Jesus. Do you know what Jesus did with the lunch before He multiplied it? He *blessed* it. He won't bless what you're ignoring.

Notice, Jesus didn't look at that lunch and say, "Is *that* all we've got? What do you expect Me to do with it?" Yet husbands and wives do that to their spouses — and we do that to God.

Jesus blessed that lunch. *Whatever you bless will multiply.* But before you bless it, you've got to *acknowledge* it. You do not ignore the things you cherish.

There are people in the world who own only one suit, and when they take it off, they carefully hang it in the closet. They take good care of it, because it's of such great value to them.

In the same way, you must take care of the things and relationships God has already supplied you. If you ignore relationships, they will deteriorate.

Jesus took the lunch, blessed it, broke it, and shared it with the multitude. Somehow that lunch went all the way around. Everyone was fed, and 12 basketfuls of food were left over!

Gather Your Crumbs!

Jesus said to His disciples, "Now gather the crumbs."
"What?"

In order to be involved in the supernatural works of God, you must be willing to not lose the blessings God has provided.

Contemporary disciples would say, "Gather the crumbs? We don't need to gather the crumbs! Everyone ate, and everyone is O.K. Why do we need to gather the crumbs?"

Jesus' instruction remains: "Gather the baskets full of crumbs."

I challenge you to look around your house. Look in your closets. Look in your garage. Look at all the things you forgot you own — all that clothing you grew out of but you're keeping in case you can fit back into it someday. Now it's stored away doing nothing.

When you look at all your unused possessions, you'll say, "My God, I'm rich!" Give these unused items away. Sow them as seed to meet people's needs. Come on, the Rapture is going to happen before you can get back into those old clothes again!

When God Is Involved

I don't have to make things work if God's in it. For example, I didn't look for my wife, Robin. God put us together. What I did not have to make happen, I don't have to keep going. It's a "done deal" if God's in it.

And it's not difficult for God to give favor to a person with an idea that will make him or her millions of dollars. But it's not going to happen to the person who is *trying* to become a millionaire.

It will probably happen to the person no one would suspect — the person who keeps busy working in the kingdom of God, doing whatever needs to be done. That person is liable to get that idea, because he's not going after it. He's just helping usher, work, and bless. Once we understand these principles, they will work for us.

When we begin to reevaluate what wealth and riches really are and we begin to work on establishing the covenant, we will go as far as we can in the supernatural provision of natural resources. We will break through into the realm of multiplication, divine favor. We will find gold in fishes' mouths!

Then we will break into a realm where God will do things that will literally change the spiritual and economic climate of a community, a city, and a nation!

Chapter 3

The Hidden Riches of the Last Days

Jesus is coming back for a Church that meets New Testament criteria. That is why average Christians today are not happy. Joy is directly linked to the success of the New Testament Church.

When you were born again, God deposited in your recreated human spirit the witness, conviction, and identity that go with His plan for His people.

Whether you know it or not, the reason some of you are not full of excitement, enthusiasm, and joy is because you prioritize insignificant things and minimize important things. I call this majoring on the minors.

The real reason for your existence as an individual believer is to bruise the head of Satan in the life of someone! After all, Jesus did it for you. You're not here just to be a victim; you're here to enforce what Jesus did and be a victor in your life and the life of someone else.

That's why the enemy is so afraid of you. That's why he works on you overtime. He doesn't work nearly as hard on the "religious" Christian who doesn't care and hasn't had an encounter with God. But when you've had an encounter with God and heard divine truth, he launches his attacks against you.

Why? He wants you to quit before you begin to realize that your vision of God is not just a fantasy; it's a reality. It's something God wants you to do. It's your destiny!

And it's not out of your reach; it's so close to you, you can literally smell it!

You are part of the generation that is going to take territory for God in these last days. You are going to make an impact. Jesus is going to come back for a victorious, triumphant Church that has made her presence known on planet Earth. *And a large part of her success is going to be financial!*

The End-Time Church: A Success

The Church of the end times is not going to be poverty-stricken, waiting for God to come and rescue her from a world system that has ruled over her and caused her to compromise. Instead, the Church is going to be successful and lack nothing!

No longer will we preach the Gospel using inferior programs and materials. We will produce the best, preach the best, and print the best, all to the glory of God. However, to accomplish that, we must understand what God is saying to us, and we must understand that this success will come about through the power of God. It's a complete change of mind-set.

On the one hand, we can't get so success-oriented that we go after success and burn ourselves out. On the other hand, we can't get so "spiritual" that we wait for a word of knowledge before we do anything.

Whatever our hands find to do, we must do with all our might, but without anxiety. And we must not do it from a defeated position, but from the superior, victorious position of someone to whom God has freely given all things.

God Our Provider

Also, we must know the reason for our success on Earth is not simply to own and possess things. We will own and have things, because God wants to take care of us.

He wants to prove Himself as our Provider so our witness and testimony will be a reality in the lives of others.

It would be ridiculous if God called Himself our Provider but never provided for us. If we told sinners, "God is the Provider," they would not believe us if He was not providing for us.

When God began to deal with me about preaching and teaching about the silver, the gold, and the glory, I found out that this mighty move of God — this mighty worldwide harvest — cannot come into its fullness unless it comes at the same level or parallel with financial increase.

For example, you can't reach people in Hollywood unless you use the right media to communicate with them, because you won't normally find them visiting a Full Gospel church. In other words, you won't be able to produce a grade-B movie about the life of Christ and reach anyone in Hollywood with it. However, I believe that in these end times God will give us ingenious revelations to fulfill our destiny and reach all people.

You're here to reach people for God, but before you can, God's got to reach you. He's got to have you before He can use you. If God doesn't have you fully, it doesn't matter what you do; you'll never be happy. Deep inside, your subconscious, the voice of your conscience, is unhappy because you're not doing what you were born to do!

If God has you fully, you can live and breathe your divine destiny. But what good is a vision you have unless God flows through you the resources necessary to fulfill your vision? Believers must understand this, because most believers will be a part of what God wants to do in the last days.

The Religious Mind Reacts

How much money can God trust the Church with? The Bible says that God owns the cattle on a thousand hills, and the Earth is the Lord's and the fullness thereof.

But the religious mind tells you, "Yes, God is sovereign and, yes, He owns everything — *but it's not for you now.* You're supposed to be *poor* now."

If this is so, why is the sovereign God seemingly funding pornography? Why does the pornographer have all the money he wants, yet the Lord owns the Earth? Why do liquor companies have all the money they need, yet God is against alcoholism?

The religious mind is so idiotic and demonic, it needs to be put out of business! Like my friend Dr. Stan McKibbon said, "You could put 90 percent of the churches in America out of business and it wouldn't do any damage to the kingdom of God."

We must understand that if God sovereignly keeps finances out of the hands of the very people who would freely give to His work, He must also sovereignly put it into the hands of those who are funding every anti-Gospel purpose. And that is the most stupid, ridiculous thing any Christian could ever say about a good God! Let's use our minds and reason this together.

A Matter of Trust

How much money does God want to flow through His people? How much of you does God want to have? Does He want just your spirit, or does He want your spirit, your mind, your body, and everything else?

Most Christians don't give themselves wholly to God because they are smart enough to know that if He keeps them poor to teach them something, and they give Him everything, including their natural efforts, they are in bad shape on planet Earth.

So without saying it, they distrust God and give Him only part of themselves — their hearts — but they live a life of saying, "I'd like to, I want to, *but....*"

If you give yourself completely to God, He will take care of you. Of course, folks in religious churches won't like you. They'll talk about you, act like you're materialistic, and so forth. They'll say you belong to a cult.

But notice, when those same churches receive an offering, they don't stop the drug addict, the gangster, or the pornographer from putting something into the offering container. And they offer no form of legitimate help to these poor people, either.

Do you know why? Because religion is not interested in multiplying it to you in good measure, pressed down, shaken together, and running over. Religion doesn't want to teach you how to multiply it. Religion just wants to take it away from you!

I'm not interested in taking what the people of God have. I'm interested in taking what the devil has, bringing it into the kingdom of God, and building the work of the kingdom with it! That's exactly what the Lord said in His Word: "...the wealth of the sinner is laid up for the just" (Proverbs 13:22).

Looking Past Cyrus to Jesus

Thus saith the Lord to his anointed, to Cyrus, whose right hand I have holden, to subdue nations before him; and I will loose the loins of kings, to open before him the two leaved gates; and the gates shall not be shut;

I will go before thee, and make the crooked places straight: I will break in pieces the gates of brass, and cut in sunder the bars of iron:

And I will give thee the treasures of darkness, and hidden riches of secret places, that thou mayest know that I, the Lord, which call thee by thy name, am the God of Israel.

For Jacob my servant's sake, and Israel mine elect, I have even called thee by thy name: I have surnamed thee, though thou hast not known me.

Isaiah 45:1-4

Anyone who knows a little bit about the Bible knows that in this passage, the prophet Isaiah was talking to Cyrus,

49

the Persian king, who was used by God to subdue and overcome nations and to spoil Babylon.

The prophet Daniel, in part of his ministry, overlapped the life and the reign of Cyrus. Most of us try to relegate this portion of scripture to a historic time, but I believe it's literally full of prophetic relevance to the present. Let me tell you why.

Whenever God says, "Thus saith the Lord to his anointed," you can bank on it that this is not referring solely to an individual who was living in Bible days. His words are spirit and life.

You can also bank on the fact that the law of double fulfillment, a prophetic law seen throughout the books of the Bible, was looking *past* Cyrus to the Anointed One, Jesus of Nazareth, whom God was going to send, give the hidden treasures, and cause to reign and take territory.

The Sun of Righteousness

This Cyrus was a courageous genius whom God used to take territory and kingdoms. His name, *Cyrus,* means "sun." Therefore, we could read Isaiah 45:1 as, "Thus saith the Lord to his anointed, to Cyrus, the sun..."

We find another important reference to "sun" in Malachi 4:2,3.

> But unto you that fear my name shall *the Sun of right-eousness* arise with healing in his wings [this refers to Jesus]; and ye shall go forth, and grow up as calves of the stall.
>
> And ye shall tread down the wicked; for they shall be ashes under the soles of your feet in the day that I shall do this, saith the Lord of hosts.

This speaks of a *spiritual* invasion. It is not referring to you and me treading wicked *people* down. It is referring to you and me treading the *forces of darkness* down as a result of the Sun of righteousness rising up with healing in His wings.

50

Not only does the Lord save you, but you grow up as "calves of the stall" before Him. That means you are well fed, well taken care of, and always provided for. That means you've become strong, because God has supplied for you. Now when you "go forth," you're no longer a victim. You tread down the forces of darkness.

The Works of the Anointed One

Looking again at Isaiah 45, notice that God called Cyrus "the anointed." Cyrus wasn't even born yet, but God called him by name in the Bible! Jesus wasn't born yet, either, but God called Him by name in the Bible.

Cyrus was the ruler of an empire. Jesus, the Anointed One, is the King of kings, and He is also the ruler of an empire, a spiritual empire.

God held Cyrus' right hand. God also held the right hand of Christ, the Sun and the Son.

Cyrus issued an edict to build the Temple in Jerusalem, and that's how Judaism started. The children of Israel were a collection of tribes until Cyrus united them into a nation and got them to build the Temple.

Stephen told us that God doesn't live within temples made with man's hands. Paul told us, *"You* are the temple of God," and "We are the house of God." Jesus said, "Upon this rock I will build My Church."

Jesus gave a prophetic edict to build the Temple, the house of God, which is made up of people who have been redeemed. The redeemed are "lively stones" or precious jewels God has brought together to form a habitation or a dwelling place for the Spirit of God on planet Earth.

This dwelling place is not found in idols, in a nice cross on the back of the platform, in a little oil displayed on the platform, in holy water in the back of the church, in a prayer bench, or in the horns of the altar. The dwelling place for the Spirit of Almighty God on planet Earth is found in the temple made up of the redeemed! To put it bluntly — in mankind!

When Christ proclaimed He is building His Church, His temple, the Church was born, and she was born in glory.

The Sun's Army

What was God going to do for this Cyrus? The Bible said He was going to loose the loins of kings. What happens when the loins of kings are loosed? Their knees smite together for fear. That's what happened to King Belshazzar when he saw the writing on the wall in Daniel 5.

Cyrus had an army. The Sun of righteousness also has an army, but some of them are AWOL and others are chubby, and they want to drop out of basic training — but He has an army nonetheless. That's why He sent some of us as drill sergeants to get you into shape.

The Sun of Righteousness' army has such a reputation, the loins of the kings of the wicked kingdom are loosed, and their knees are smiting together, because the devil also believes and trembles!

The Enemy Called "Religion"

Do you know what the devil's main ally is? *Religion.* A pastor friend of mine in Rhode Island shared this interesting story with me.

Four young people in a Christian band came out of a long-established Full Gospel denominational church that rejected them, and they began attending his church.

They had been thoroughly indoctrinated in religion while attending that denominational church. Then they became turned off to their church once they became Christian musicians.

They had long hair, and they were playing heavy metal music — but they were playing in some unusual places, and they had altar calls and led people to the Lord.

Even so, most pastors don't want weird-looking kids like that who wear leather and earrings, have long hair, and play that kind of music attending their church.

And that's precisely what is wrong with the Church: *The Church today doesn't know how to reach the world.* You could rapture the Church as it is, and most of the world wouldn't miss it.

Offended by the Move of God

My pastor friend took these kids in. It made them very happy to have a pastor who would minister to them and accept them just the way they were. However, the kids got *offended* because people in his congregation were dancing in the Spirit!

These head-banging, bead-wearing, long-haired, heavy metal Pentecostal kids couldn't handle *dancing* in the church because of their religious upbringing!

The pastor said to them, "Wait a minute! Let me get this straight. I received *you* just the way you are, and you've got a problem with my people dancing in church?"

What happened to those young people for them to act that way? Religion, the ally of Satan, influenced them early in life and indoctrinated them to be non-relevant, non-impacting, non-influential non-players in the world. They didn't know what would stop evil.

Go With the Flow

I have another pastor friend whose church started flowing in revival, but some of the teenagers remained like bumps on a log, not wanting to get into the Spirit.

Their parents came to the pastor and said, "When are you going to get over this thing and get back to the way things were?"

The pastor said, "I'm *never* going back to the way things were!"

The parents left and took their teenagers somewhere else.

It has become obvious to me that the kids are leading the parents. If the parents are following the next generation, it ought to be a clue to us who the next leaders of this world are.

Let's reach the kids. Most want revival, and the same parents who cater to their backsliding will cater to their on-fire experience with God, because religion has taught them to "go with the flow." In other words, go with whatever is popular.

You're part of an army, and the terror and fear of you has fallen on the kings in the kingdom of darkness, and their knees are shaking. The next step is, grow up and go out to start treading the wicked under your feet. And part of the treading is *financial treading!*

Changing the Tide

Isaiah 45:1 says the two-leaved gates will be opened to Cyrus. The *Taylor* translation says, "God shall open the gates of Babylon to him. The gates shall not be shut against him anymore."

Before Cyrus was born, God prophesied about him. Why? Because He had someone anointed who was going to come and change the tide of the ruling power and the superpower in the world known as Babylon.

Babylon is both lost and religious. She's on her way to hell, but she's going there *religiously*. Although Babylon is a religious system, she is also a worldly system and a very rich kingdom.

The gates of Babylon were going to be opened wide so the army of the Sun of righteousness could walk in and plunder her, taking her gold, silver, and precious stones to build the Temple of the house of the Lord.

Get a clue as to why we're here. *Realize there are open gates waiting for us to invade!* The Church wants to "hold the fort," but we need to go to plunder Babylon. God has opened the gates of Babylon for us, and we should walk in there in the anointing.

Spiritual Versus Sentimental

If more people would become *spiritual* rather than *sentimental*, we would empty "the synagogues of Satan" — the religious churches — in a very short period of time. However, some people love the pew they're sitting on so much, they contribute to that "synagogue of Satan" because their parents attended there. They are sentimental about it.

Most people would rather pat you on the back than lay hands on you with the anointing and cast the devil off you. Most people sit in the same pew their grandpa sat in. Most people cry at the same phrase every time a certain song is sung. Religion stinks! Why do you think they call the seats "pews"?

They grew up religiously, and they contribute in the offering containers of Babylon to keep the wealth within the gates that have already been opened. The King has already made the way smooth for us to plunder the gold, the silver, and the glory of Babylon.

We're here to tell the captives of Babylon, "Come out of Babylon! It's time to rebuild the Temple of the Lord and make a habitation of God for the Spirit in the Earth realm!"

Now I am going to prophesy something to you. There are churches right now that are governing in the Spirit, but it doesn't seem like it in the natural, because spiritual authority cannot be measured by numbers.

Do you understand you can have 5000 members in your church but have zero power in the Spirit realm? If one can put a thousand to flight when he is in faith, and two can put 10,000 to flight when they are in faith as a power of agreement, what do you think *negative agreement* will achieve? How about 5000 people committed to failure on planet Earth?

The Religious Order Is Dying

In the next few years, we will see the failure of these religious churches and institutions. It will look like it happened overnight, but it didn't.

The dead religious order of Babylon may look good on the *outside*, and some of its leaders may think it's "business as usual," but inspect *beneath* the surface and you will find that demonic "termites" have been eating away at the very foundations. The gates are open, and the spoil is coming out!

"I will go before you and make the rough places smooth; I will shatter the doors of bronze, and cut through their iron bars" is how the *New American Standard Version* translates Isaiah 45:2. *The New English Bible* says, "The bronze doors will I shatter, and the iron gates will I snap."

Do you know what purpose the bronze doors and the iron gates serve? They keep the wealth of Babylon inside Babylon, and it's difficult getting in there. But the good news is, God is making the rough places smooth for the army of Cyrus to enter. How? God always "speaks" to places and changes them.

Smoothing the Path

Even in the time of John the Baptist, God spoke to the high mountains to come down and the crooked places to be straightened. God was a voice crying in the wilderness, "Prepare ye the way of the Lord, make his paths straight" (Luke 3:4). He has been speaking through His anointed prophets and preachers about this for many generations, all along smoothing the path of the Church.

Therefore, transition is going to be smoother than you think. God will snap the gates and break the bars. He is going to make the crooked places straight, smooth the rough places, break the gates of brass in pieces, and shatter the iron bars. Isaiah 45:3 says, "And I will give thee the treasures of darkness, and hidden riches of secret places, that thou mayest know that I, the Lord, which call thee by thy name, am the God of Israel."

What *are* the treasures of darkness? This is one mistake the Church makes. Whenever we hear the word "darkness," we immediately think it's associated with the devil and his works.

"Hoarded Wealth of Secret Places"

In this case, we think, "Treasures of darkness means it's connected to the kingdom of darkness." However, the *Berkeley* translation says, "I am going to give you the hoarded wealth of secret places."

Another translation says, "Treasures that are hidden in darkness." The *Knox* translation says, "Their hidden treasures, their most secret hoards, I will hand over to thee." I love the Knox translation!

The Book of James refers to fields that were kept back by fraud (James 5:4). James wrote, "...You have heaped to yourselves treasures for the last days" (James 5:3). Just imagine: Hidden treasures, fields, and abundance have been held back from the kingdom of God by fraud!

This is because the devil claimed it and lied to Christians about their ownership of it; and the Christians believed religion, the ally of the devil, and went ahead without what was rightfully theirs as the Gospel suffered.

The Winning Team

But the Church is going to win. We're on the winning team — and Jesus owns the team! Anytime you own a winning team, you make money.

The winning team doesn't know the gates have been broken, and the hidden treasures are available. All they need is to learn how to cooperate with the Spirit of God who is moving in the Earth realm.

Daniel 2:22 refers to God: "He revealeth the deep and secret things: he knoweth what is in the darkness, and the light dwelleth with him."

God reveals the deep and the secret things, and He knows what is in the darkness. Not only does that mean that God sees what people can't see regarding sin and hidden things; it also means He has knowledge of what has not yet been revealed to mankind.

So where is it hidden? It is hidden in that realm of revelation. Man doesn't have revelation of it yet, so he doesn't even know it exists. There are countless hidden things. We know this because awesome technologies are being discovered or invented every day.

Fighting Progress

Religion, the ally of Satan, is against progressive revelation. Let me give you an example. By 1900, the Holy Ghost had been operating in the Earth realm for almost two thousand years. At that time, some Christians got hold of the fact that He is for today, and they began to pray for the Holy Ghost. They consequently were baptized in the Holy Ghost and started praying with other tongues.

Religion said, "They're fools! It's not biblical! It's not of God! They're going to hell!" You can trace their attitude down through the following decades. Some of you were part of the booming Charismatic Movement that developed. But when you started dancing in the Spirit, much of the traditional Pentecostal community fought it. That's because religion is anti-progressive revelation. Religion wants things to stay the way they used to be.

Religion knows that once you learn the truth, the truth will make you free. But if you're anti-revelation, you're pro-darkness. Whatever is not revealed is not revealed either because it's not in the light, or there's no light on it yet. It's still unrevealed.

What kind of a person would say, "No, we don't want to discover the cures to any diseases"? That would be ridiculous, yet Christians say, "No, don't dig into the Word of God and find out anything relevant to us right now. We know it all."

What do you know?

"We know that we don't know everything, but we're going to know it one day. That's what we know. We know that we don't know why God does things the way He does."

Some people don't know anything, and they're satisfied with their lack of knowledge. They're being foolish, yet they want to be leaders. They need to get a job!

Satan's Limitations

God reveals the deep and secret things. He knows what is in the darkness. If He knows what is in the darkness, He is capable of shedding light on it. And if God sheds light on what has not been illuminated before, you can get a revelation of its existence, and then you have access to its provisions.

There are valuable things in the Earth realm that Satan remains unaware of because he is not a creator, and God hasn't yet shed light on how the people of God can use these things. The treasures of darkness are treasures I don't think Satan knows about. We give him much more credit than he deserves.

We can see what an idiot Satan really is just from looking at society during the Dark Ages to the day when Martin Luther said, "The just shall live by faith" which, by the way, was a revelation that mankind hadn't had before, even though it is found in Scripture.

In fact, until that time in history, mankind had discovered little of scientific, technological, or medical significance. All revelatory knowledge comes from the Word of God anyway. Satan has nothing whatsoever to offer. He's in so much darkness, he can't even see! All he can do is imitate what God has created.

An Outpouring of Knowledge

Since the turn of the 20th century — when the modern-day outpouring of the Holy Ghost occurred — until today, nearly 100 years later, mankind has experienced an awesome leap in knowledge.

What happened was that the Holy Ghost has been extremely active in the Earth, and even people who were not filled with the Holy Ghost were able somehow to tap into some of the provisions of the Spirit of God.

We give the devil too much credit for discoveries. People say, "The devil invented TV." The devil never invented TV. He just realized it was a good idea to control it. We are beginning to take the airwaves back.

God knows what is in the darkness. That means He can always shed light on it, and when He does, we have access to it. That's why the greatest treasure to have is the Bible and the Spirit of Truth, who is able to unfold the Word to you. It makes you wealthy before you ever own a cent.

When we refer to silver, gold, glory, and wealth, we are also referring to *spiritual wealth*. What are you going to do with your money if you are *spiritually poor?* You'll misuse it, and it will inevitably control you.

Revealed Things

We have established that God knows what is in the darkness, and the light dwells with Him. Deuteronomy 29:29 speaks of the secret things:

> **The secret things belong unto the Lord our God: but those things which are revealed belong unto us and to our children for ever, that we may do all the words of this law.**

The hidden things or the secret things belong to whom? God. The hidden things don't belong to the devil, but the revealed things belong to us. Do you know what is revealed? Whatever light is shining on and whatever you've got insight into belongs to you and your children.

This means, *if you've got insight into it, it's yours!* That's why I'd rather sit under a ministry that has revelation. I know they've got whatever they have revelation on.

We say the secret things belong to God, but what are those secret things? Whatever is in the darkness. Why? Because there is no light shining on them. Even so, God knows what is in that darkness. Because He is such a good God, He reserves the deep and the secret things for certain dispensations, and then He reveals them to fuel prophetic words.

Divine Ideas

All of a sudden, the treasure of something that existed all along comes into the open and becomes available for the people of God. And when His people get that revelation, it is right on time.

The treasure had been in the darkness, but the devil hadn't known about it, because he was "in the dark" about it.

The secret things belong to God, but the revealed things belong to us and our children. God takes the secret things and reveals them to us. Why? He wants to give them to us and our children so we may do all the words of this law.

If you combine this truth with Deuteronomy 8:18 — which says it is God who gives you the power to get wealth, that He may establish His covenant which He swore — you find that *the power to get wealth is the fact that God reveals and makes accessible to you what you did not know before.* It is the truth that sets you free!

You can be sitting somewhere minding your own business, and a divine idea can come and help you in any area of life whatsoever — from a small idea on how to deal with your kids all the way to a major scientific break-through.

Divine ideas come as a result of revelation. Revelation comes as a result of the entrance of God's Word, which gives light and gives understanding to the simple. Revelation also comes as a result of an open heaven. And an open heaven comes as a result of an acceptable offering.

Hindrances to Blessing

Religion preaches giving and tithing, but most religious churches will not go out on a limb and promise that God will multiply your gift and pay you back and bless you.

They hide behind the religious "cloak" that piously says, "We don't give because we want something in return. We give because we love." What they are really saying is, "We just want your money, but we don't want to be responsible for your lack of results."

When the child of God gives and tithes offering after offering but God does not respond, there must be a reason, because God is not a liar. Preachers and teachers should know the reason so they can teach people how to stop giving without receiving and get to the place where they are blessed by God.

One reason why God doesn't respond to an offering is when it is not an *acceptable* offering. Abel's offering was acceptable. He brought the fat, the riches, and the firstlings of his flock, which means he put God first.

Cain's offering, on the other hand, was not acceptable. The Bible says, "Cain brought also his vegetables." You can see how Abel took the offering seriously and offered it to God with his whole heart, whereas Cain had a different motivation. God gave honor to Abel rather than Cain.

God's Blessing

People don't understand that you can tithe religiously, but if your heart is far from God, He can't get His blessings over to you, simply because you are not walking in the Spirit. Most of His blessings come in the form of divine ideas or accuracy and excellency in what you do.

For example, if you're a salesman, your results depend on whether you knock on all the right doors or all the wrong doors.

People have said, "I've tried tithing, and it just doesn't work." They probably plopped some unacceptable offering in the bucket. They're still living their lives in the same old compromising way, yet they think they're going to hear from a holy God — but it just doesn't work that way.

However, once they "get with the program," all those hidden things — the ideas, the divine revelations, and the small alignments that make major impacts — will begin to happen in their lives.

A New Covenant

As we previously saw, God said, "...those things which are revealed belong unto us and to our children for ever...." (Deuteronomy 29:29). If you combine that verse with Deuteronomy 8:18, which says that God gives you the power to get wealth so that He may establish His covenant, you tie that into what the covenant is. As God reveals His secret things to His children, He is giving us the power to establish His covenant.

Just what is the covenant that you can establish through wealth? God tells us in Jeremiah 31:31-33:

> Behold, the days come, saith the Lord, that I will make a new covenant with the house of Israel and with the house of Judah:
>
> Not according to the covenant that I made with their fathers in the day that I took them by the hand to bring them out of the land of Egypt...
>
> But this shall be the covenant that I will make with the house of Israel; After those days, saith the Lord, I will put my law in their inward parts, and write it in their hearts; and will be their God, and they shall be my people.

The reason for the establishment of the covenant is to get the Word into the hearts and minds of God's people.

First, a preacher is needed who has the Word of God and does not preach "religion" as the ally of Satan. Second, the preacher must sow the Word of God into the hearts of people. His actions will be limited by the resources in his life and the lives of those who already have the Word of God established in their spirits and minds.

In order to establish the covenant in the Earth and get the law of God written in the hearts and the minds of multitudes upon multitudes, we must use the power to get wealth, the power God gave us so we could establish that covenant in the Earth — the covenant of converting millions upon millions of people to the Lord Jesus Christ through healings, signs, wonders, casting out devils, and so forth.

The kingdom of God will be involved in massive productions to get people saved. That's why establishing the covenant God swore must be done through wealth. The wealth is out there. Some of it is hidden treasure, but God will reveal it so it belongs to us and our children.

God's Word says that every good and perfect gift comes from above, from the Father of lights. He is the Father of lights, because He is the One who shines light upon the treasure. I never saw that before, and it was right under my nose all along!

"Well, I gave, but it didn't work." Can you tithe and give diligently and it not work? Yes. The Bible tells us, "Ye ask, and receive not, because ye ask amiss, that ye may consume it upon your lusts" (James 4:3).

Treasure that is hidden may be hidden for a reason; for example, because God doesn't want someone with the wrong motive to have it. So someone with the wrong motives who wants to consume the treasure on his lusts won't get anything, even though he's tithing. Why? Because prosperity is not for our own lusts! You could tithe wrong. You could give wrong. You could ask amiss. All of these will close the windows of blessing.

But if you know the purpose for your existence, you could say, "God, I want more than my needs met. Otherwise, my purpose is not fulfilled. You didn't create me to fend for myself anyway." Then God starts pouring His blessings through you so that you can establish the covenant. God doesn't mind your having money or things. But don't forget, God is not mocked. He can easily see your motives.

Qualifying for the Blessings

Now let's return to Isaiah 45:3.

And I will give thee the treasures of darkness, and hidden riches of secret places, that thou mayest know that I, the Lord, which call thee by thy name, am the God of Israel.

I expect you to prosper, increase, get blessed, and take some of it back to your church. Furthermore, I expect these blessings to continue to work in your life until the Rapture!

It is God's will for these works of His to happen to His anointed people all over planet Earth. And there is a way you can qualify for these blessings.

I want to show you in Ezra what happens to you supernaturally in the most natural way if you meet these qualifications. In the first verses of Ezra 1 we read:

Now in the first year of Cyrus king of Persia, that the word of the Lord by the mouth of Jeremiah might be fulfilled, the Lord stirred up the spirit of Cyrus king of Persia, that he made a proclamation throughout all his kingdom, and put it also in writing, saying,

Thus saith Cyrus king of Persia, The Lord God of heaven hath given me all the kingdoms of the earth; and he hath charged me to build him an house at Jerusalem, which is in Judah.

Ezra 1:1,2

Do you see it? When it came time to fulfill Jeremiah's word, which was really God's Word, to build the Temple, the one who ruled the kingdoms, Cyrus (Sun) — the Sun who ruled the kingdoms — said, "God has given me the kingdoms. Now I'm putting this in writing. Build the house of God!"

A Word for Today

This is how this passage from Ezra affects you and me:

Who is there among you of all his people? his God be with him, and let him go up to Jerusalem, which is in Judah, and build the house of the Lord God of Israel, (he is the God,) which is in Jerusalem.

And whosoever remaineth in any place where he sojourneth [or travels], let the men of his place help him with silver, and with gold, and with goods, and with beasts, beside the freewill offering for the house of God that is in Jerusalem.

Ezra 1:3,4

If you have faith, you should take this as your legitimate contract for planet Earth. This is a decree from the One decreeing that the house of the Lord be built. We have a responsibility to establish the covenant.

The decree is this: Besides the offering taken up in the house of the Lord, let every one of you who sojourns (travels) be conscious of the fact that *people are going to give you silver, gold, goods, and cars.* Cars are the modern equivalent of the beasts of the Old Testament. People, even non-Christians, are going to give you these things!

Strengthened To Build God's House

You need to bear in mind while you're working on the job and going about your daily activities that you, too, are on your way to Jerusalem to build the house of the Lord!

Then rose up the chief of the fathers of Judah and Benjamin, and the priests, and the Levites, with all them whose spirit God had raised, to go up to build the house of the Lord which is in Jerusalem.

And all they that were about them strengthened their hands with vessels of silver, with gold, with goods, with beasts, with precious things, beside all that was willingly offered.

Also Cyrus the king brought forth the vessels of the house of the Lord, which Nebuchadnezzar had brought forth out of Jerusalem, and had put them in the house of his gods;

Even those did Cyrus king of Persia bring forth by the hand of Mithredath the treasurer, and numbered them unto Sheshbazzar, the prince of Judah.

And this is the number of them: thirty chargers of gold, a thousand chargers of silver, nine and twenty knives,

Thirty basons of gold, silver basons of a second sort four hundred and ten, and other vessels a thousand.

All the vessels of gold and of silver were five thousand and four hundred. All these did Sheshbazzar bring up with them of the captivity that were brought up from Babylon unto Jerusalem.

Ezra 1:5-11

Other than the freewill offerings the people gave, every sojourner heading back to Jerusalem to fulfill his destiny by rebuilding the house of God that was broken down — the thing that had been ravaged by religion and the onslaughts of doctrines of devils — was helped and strengthened liberally by the people around him. It's a natural thing to build God's Temple and establish His covenant!

Not only that, but everything the the devil had stolen from the Temple — all the Temple vessels — and transported to Babylon were restored to the Jews and returned to the Temple in Jerusalem!

A Prophetic Picture of the Church

I see that as the perfect prophetic picture of the Church in these last days. Get ready for your hands to be strengthened with the abundance necessary for us to build the house of the Lord!

We are going to build everything God tells us to build. It will never become a task or a pressure on the people of God, and we will never go without. We are always going to have more than we need to fulfill what God has called us to fulfill, in the mighty Name of Jesus!

Does your heart burn to build the house of the Lord? Do you want to see the Law — the Word of God, the word of faith — written on the hearts and the minds of people all over the globe? Do you want to run into Christians everywhere you turn?

If that is your motivation, get ready — because people are getting ready to strengthen your hands with gold, silver, and abundance!

Prayer

Lord, we want to build the habitation of God; not a building or a project. We want to build up Christians. We want to build up the Church. We want to see the Word of God multiplied.

We recognize the edict that the King of kings and the Lord of lords, the Possessor of heaven and Earth, has already written. This New Testament of blessing says He has redeemed us from the curse of the Law, that the blessing of Abraham might come on the Gentiles through Jesus Christ, that we might receive the promise of the Spirit through faith.

We thank You right now for silver. We thank You for gold. We thank you for prosperity and increase. We vow to give You glory as we are journeying to build the house of God every moment of every day.

The sales will come, the contracts will be written, the promotion will come, the settlement will be loosed, the abundance will be given, and the inheritance will be received. The blessings and the provisions will come, in the mighty Name of Jesus!

Chapter 4

Revelation Produces Wealth

There has never been a day like this one! I feel in my heart and know in my spirit that we are part of a "departure." I'm not even referring to leaving planet Earth, although when the Rapture occurs, we'll be among the first to go.

What I am referring to is departing from man's ways and religious ways of doing things. I know beyond a shadow of a doubt we are part of this departure.

You can tap in to God in such a way that it gets better and better each time, and you go deeper and deeper until you no longer know how to go back to the way things used to be.

The reason most religious Christians don't do so is because they have been set up by religion to keep going in circles. They celebrate Christmas and New Year's, and then they go on to celebrate Easter. Later, it's time for Thanksgiving and Christmas again.

Most of the time when the Spirit of God begins to move, these Christians are already caught up in a certain momentum, and their minds are focussed on times and seasons.

Under such circumstances, it is difficult for God to break into their seasonal acknowledgments. If they won't allow Him to move in their lives, they end up reverting back to their old ways of doing things.

The Bible calls it observing times and seasons and new moons and sabbaths and holidays. And we have been set free from that!

How many of you have ever thought, "I can't do that — it's Christmastime!" Some even question, "Should we celebrate Christmas?"

There is nothing wrong with celebrating Christmas, Easter, or other holidays unless your whole life is centered around them. But the average religious person looks at the calendar and says, "Oh, I can't do that then, because it's Secretaries Day," or "God can't do that then, because it's Veterans Day." The calendar is telling us when God might be able to do something in our lives, and when it's out of the question for Him to do something in our lives.

Living on "Automatic"

Many of us were raised in Christian circles, and it's easy for us to fall into a religious "routine" where we don't even have to think about what we are doing. We automatically worship God, pray, work, go home, go to church, and so forth.

But when we get hooked up with the Holy Ghost, we must establish new and better patterns, knowing that things can change for the better, and routine is never again to be the controlling factor in our lives.

After I got turned on to God, there were times I forgot my own birthday! There have been times my wife and I remembered our anniversary that night as we were preaching somewhere. You can get so caught up in God, your calendar no longer dictates who you are or what day it is.

As a child of God living in the last days, you must realize that there is a wisdom that is far greater than a calendar, and there is a way of the Spirit that is better and greater than the religious way of doing things.

God's Intention for Us

We must understand that we are part of a final move of the Spirit of God, and He intends to bless each of us abundantly above what we can dream, envision, or imagine.

It is God's intention for us to step into the realm of benefit provision and supernatural increase, because supernatural increase is the wealth that is supposed to help us establish the covenant.

We found out from the Word of God that when something is hidden in darkness, it is hidden because there is no light of revelation revealing it. That's where ideas come from.

We have also noticed that since the Holy Spirit was poured out at Azusa Street, mankind — even in the secular community — has made tremendous breakthroughs in such areas as medicine and technology. Some of these technologies were designed by God to be a contribution to the last-day revival.

Do you know the Bible says that when Christ returns, every eye shall see Him? Jesus likened that to lightning lighting up the whole sky. Some will dismiss this, reasoning that lightning only lights up the sky you are living under; it doesn't light the other side of the globe.

But God, through His Spirit, gave people the ability to invent technology that gave us television and satellites so every eye on planet Earth will be able to see the Second Coming of the Lord Jesus Christ when He returns in His glory with His saints!

We must also understand that the printing press was really invented so the Bible could be widely distributed to every person and every home. God gave someone the concept for the printing press because it was no longer efficient for scribes to laboriously copy the Bible letter by letter and word by word.

A World Outreach

It is not God's will for certain cults to use the printing press to disseminate their literature. I think the Church should have more money than any other community on planet Earth, religious or otherwise, so we can give books or sermons to people, and we can visit their homes and witness to them, regardless of where they are in the world.

For us to be able to do these things, God must get money to us. God is not going to use someone who doesn't care about Him to preach His Gospel. Therefore, He will give us the hidden treasures to use for the work of the kingdom. For us to receive those hidden treasures, we must use the power He gave us.

As we saw in the previous chapter, the Bible says, "But thou shalt remember the Lord thy God: for it is he that giveth thee power to get wealth, that he may establish his covenant which he sware unto thy fathers, as it is this day" (Deuteronomy 8:18).

God's New Covenant

How will God establish His covenant? Hebrews 8 speaks of the covenant God is now making with His people.

...Behold, the days come, saith the Lord, when I will make a new covenant with the house of Israel and with the house of Judah.

Not according to the covenant that I made with their fathers in the day when I took them by the hand to lead them out of the land of Egypt; because they continued not in my covenant, and I regarded them not, saith the Lord

For this is the covenant that I will make with the house of Israel after those days, saith the Lord; I will put my laws into their mind, and write them in their hearts; and I will be to them a God, and they shall be to me a people.

Hebrews 8:8-10

So basically, the sown, preached, taught, published Word is being inscribed by His divine Spirit upon the hearts and the minds of men and women. Now they are full of the Word of God and the Spirit of God.

When they encounter the world, the world sees in them a contract between God and man; a commitment between God and man to work together. They see God at work through the Christian. God called that the covenant.

Do you know why there are people on Earth who are still worshipping a piece of wood or a piece of gold? Do you want to know why there is still idolatry on planet Earth?

Sad to say, sometimes in Full Gospel churches people idolize their finances, their goals, their careers, and their plans more than they do God. Some pastors idolize their programs more than they do God. The Holy Ghost can't move because of their program. That makes the program the god of their service.

How To Reach the Unreachable

The Spirit of God has not finished writing the Word of God on the hearts and the minds of people. In fact, He has barely gotten started. There are some people He cannot reach, because missionaries or preachers still can't get to them and minister effectively.

There are places in North America where conventional ways of preaching the Gospel won't work. There are kids who won't listen to conventional ways of preaching the Gospel because of the devil's influence. He has successfully launched accusations against born-again, Spirit-filled Christians in certain levels of society, making "Christian" a derogatory term.

To reach these groups, we will need an ingenious idea, a divine calling, and a supernatural financial deposit so we can produce and take the best to them. Then, before they know what hit them, they will be praying the sinner's prayer and receiving Jesus Christ as their Savior!

Our new church building in Pensacola, Florida, is going to look like a coffee shop on the outside. It will contain a Christian bookstore, a gym, a martial arts studio, a cappuccino bar, and an auditorium, among other things.

People can walk in and sit there, and they will be sitting in the same glory that is in the services held in the auditorium. They won't even know what is going on.

They will just know they walked in full of anxiety, but they had a cappuccino, read a little book, or maybe talked to someone, and now they feel at peace. Before they know it, they are addicted to the atmosphere. Then they are going to see the auditorium and know it is a church.

Revelation Brings Riches

God is going to give us the hidden treasures. They are in the Earth, but they are still hidden.

The average child of God needs to understand that when we are Spirit-led, we are led into all truth, and those ideas will change our lives forever.

The moment a revelation starts working, riches are the result. For example, we were poverty-stricken spiritually before we met Jesus. Spiritually speaking, we were poor, naked, and blind. Then we got a revelation on salvation. When we got that revelation, we became spiritually rich!

Revelation produces instantaneous wealth, because God never reveals anything insignificant. Everything God reveals is a gift for man. How do we know this? Deuteronomy 29:29 says, "The secret things belong unto the Lord our God: but those things which are revealed belong unto us and to our children for ever, that we may do all the words of this law."

God is in the business of taking what is hidden and revealing it. Why? Because every good and perfect gift comes above, from the Father of lights. He shines His lights on one of His hidden things and brings what He calls revelation and insight. You see it and say, "You mean that's mine?" You receive it. Now you're richer than you were before you received it.

If God wants you to have something, He must reveal it first, because only what is revealed belongs to you. As long as it's hidden, it's His.

Guess what God does? He sends you a preacher who saw the revelation. He starts preaching the revelation to you, and once you see it, what you see belongs to you by virtue of the principles of the Word of God. Once you see it, it's yours!

Treasures of Riches

Once we knew about salvation, we became instantaneously spiritually rich. However, if we say that salvation is foolishness, or the message of the Gospel is crazy, we won't receive the riches of it. But if we believe it, we'll receive the riches of it.

We also become wealthy in the natural realm through revelation. For example, I was once a drug addict, but when I found out that the anointing of God would break drug addiction off my physical and psychological life, I had the wealth of it. I had access to it, and it broke my bondage.

The same principle is relevant to the person who is dying with AIDS or the person who has multiple sclerosis or any other disease. The moment they see that Christ is the Healer and they receive this revelation, they become physically rich. They are healed and enjoy divine health.

So there are treasures of riches in the spiritual area, the intellectual area, the physical area, and the financial area that belong to the child of God.

A Different Kind of Bondage

I've lived in Christian circles for some years now. Actually, I've lived in Christian circles all my life in one sense, because I grew up Catholic. I went to church regularly when I was a little kid.

When I came to America, I found out that you need to get born again. I got saved, and I became involved with a group of people I felt were free from the yoke of religious bondage — until I learned better and found out that Full Gospel people are just as religious as some Catholics are! They just have different bondages than the Catholics do.

As I began to dig into the Word of God, I found out that some of the things we believed and built our faith on were not things we were supposed to build our faith on.

For example, I heard many sermons on "What We Don't Know." I heard preachers say, "Well, my brother, we know in part, we prophesy in part, and now we see through a glass darkly."

Why Concentrate on the Ditch?

If you were driving your car through a powerful storm, your windshield wipers were working hard, and you had enough light to see what was in front of you, would you concentrate on the ditch and say, "My God, I don't know why we can't see what's going on over there — but we will in the sweet by-and-by."

Friend, the sweet by-and-by will come sooner than you think if you concentrate on what you cannot see, because God didn't call us to preach what we can't see!

Even "through a glass darkly" we see *something*, and if we don't see clearly, we just go a little slower; but we do get to where we're going, because there is more than zero visibility. We don't preach what we don't see; we preach what we do see.

I found out that we were majoring in what we don't know. Since the hidden things don't belong to us, why even talk about them?

Sometimes when you tell people that it is God's will for us to be healthy, they ask, "Yeah, but what about so-and-so, who's got such-and-such disease?" Forget about the car in the ditch! You need to focus all your energy on what you can see in order to stay on the road on which God is directing you.

Preaching the "Good News"

God sent us to preach what we have revelation on. I started preaching what I know, and people said, "He's arrogant. He acts like he knows it all." Yes, I know it all — I know everything I know. That's all I'm preaching, anyway. If I preached what I know and claimed I didn't know it, that would be stupidity by design.

Religion immediately pulls back, puts up a shield, and says, "They act like they know it all!" — just because you're preaching what you know. How can what you're preaching be called "good news" if you're not sure it's the truth? Preach what you know.

Yes, we know in part. I've got a part, and I'm preaching the part I know. You also have a part. I know my part well, and I'm growing in my knowledge of my part. I study to show myself approved to God when I'm preaching that part.

I find that my part grows if I'm faithful in my part, because whatever is revealed belongs to me. Why should I concentrate on what is *not* revealed if what is revealed is sufficient?

Choose Life

God said to us in Deuteronomy 30:19, "I call heaven and earth to record this day against you, that I have set before you life and death, blessing and cursing: therefore choose life, that both thou and thy seed may live."

God is referring to both eternal life and abundant life. The Bible says abundant life is what Jesus came to give us. Jesus said, "The thief cometh not, but for to steal, and to kill, and to destroy: I am come that they might have life, and that they might have it more abundantly" (John 10:10).

That tells me two things: First, that Christ is in the business of giving me abundant life; second, the presence

77

of abundant life is the absence of theft, murder, and destruction that are a direct result of the work of Satan.

If I accept abundant life into my life, I am going to be putting the thief out of commission, because I will know he's the one that comes to steal, kill, and destroy. I'm not going to receive anything he brings; I'm only going to receive what the light of God's revelation is bringing — eternal and abundant life.

Walking in the Light

The Bible also tells us to walk in the light. This means we are to walk in both eternal life and abundant life. How do we know that? Because "In him was life; and the life was the light of men" (John 1:4).

If I walk in the light, what is the light? The light is what is revealed. If I walk in what is revealed to me, I have fellowship with God, and I stay away from what is in darkness. Therefore, I should stay in the realm where I see and know in order to have eternal and abundant life operating in me.

As we saw in Deuteronomy 30, God has placed before us life and death, blessing and cursing, asking us to choose between them. We will choose according to our mind-set and our determination to concentrate on one of the two spectrums.

We can choose to be pessimistic, downcast Christians who always say, "We don't know," because we're fear- and curse-oriented; or we can choose to be children of faith who focus on what God has revealed, saying, "We know everything we need to know," concentrating on blessing and life.

When I get into the area of financial blessing, I am in the area of God's provision. Why? Because God gave the revelation of Himself and called Himself Jehovah-Jireh, the Provider. He called Himself "the God who is more than enough." If I have a revelation of that, what is revealed belongs to me.

The God who is more than enough in my life belongs to me and my children, so I will step into the arena of having more than enough in my life and the lives of my children.

When the Word of the Lord Is Rare

To show you how this works and where the Church is in relation to it, look at First Samuel 3. From this we will see what kind of a day Samuel lived in.

The first verse says, "...And the word of the Lord was precious in those days; there was no open vision." This doesn't mean that the Word of the Lord was precious in the sense of being "priceless"; it means the Word of the Lord was *rare*. And wherever the Word of the Lord is rare, there is no revelation.

Why? Because the entrance of the Word gives life, revelation, or insight; and wherever there is ignorance of the Word, there is ignorance of the will of God and an absence of His blessings, because there is no access to the blessings.

If the Word of God is rare, and you're not hearing it, whatever God is revealing is not being revealed to you, because it must come to you through the entrance of His Word into your life.

Restrain Your Life

That is why God said, "My people are destroyed for lack of knowledge..." (Hosea 4:6). Another translation says, "My people cast off restraint because of a lack of knowledge or without a vision, rather, the people cast off restraint."

If you're without a vision, you're without knowledge. And without knowledge of the will of God, you won't restrain your life through faith to go in the direction where there is light. You will allow yourself to float without direction. But God wants us to restrain our lives.

How do you restrain your life financially? By living right, obeying the Scriptures about tithing and giving, and being good stewards over your finances. You can also restrain it with your confession regarding your finances.

Don't plop your offering in the bucket and leave the church, saying, "I wonder..." No, keep your confession in line and in agreement with blessing, regardless of how long it takes to see it manifested.

Preaching the Curse

So the Word of God was precious or rare in Samuel's day, and it's just as precious in these days. For example, when preachers tell you it's the will of God for you to be sick, that's murder! That's anarchy! There is no excuse for preaching the curse from the pulpit!

It is not the will of God for you to be poverty-stricken. It is not the will of God for you to be sick. It is not the will of your heavenly Father for you to go through hell on planet Earth!

God is a better Father than human fathers. He said, "If human fathers will not give their children that which is evil, how much more will your heavenly Father give the Holy Ghost to those that ask Him?" (See Luke 11:13.)

The Word of God is precious today, and I am committed to what it says. Of course, the devil will always ask you, "But what about this or that situation?"

Tell him that until God gives you a revelation about that situation, you are not even going to grace it with talk or confession. Tell him you've only got revelation on what God said, and that's all you're going to believe.

Did you know God is not going to give you a word or a revelation that you're not ready to believe yet? When I get to heaven, I'm going to be judged by what I did with what I know now. It's not the truth that sets you free but what you do with the truth! We believers should look at the Word that God has revealed to us and believe it in spite of our circumstance.

Rehashed Sermons

The Word of God was rare, and there was no open vision in the time of Samuel. It was a hectic time. The old priest Eli got fat, became backslidden, wouldn't correct his family, and "laid down in his place" or slept.

Eli hadn't seen a vision or heard a revelation from God for years! He was preaching rehashed sermons, using the same notes he'd had for years. And he could not see, either literally or spiritually.

First Samuel 1:3 says, "And ere the lamp of God went out in the temple of the Lord...." It's terrible when the Church's lamp has gone out!

One night, the Lord called Samuel's name. Verse 4 tells us that young Samuel replied, "Here am I." And he ran to Eli, thinking the old priest had called him. But Eli told him, "Go lie down. I didn't call you."

The Lord called Samuel again, and again he ran to Eli and said, "You called me." Eli replied, "I didn't call you. Go lie down."

Now look at verse 7: "Now Samuel did not yet know the Lord, neither was the word of the Lord yet revealed unto him."

The State of the Church

Do you know where the Church of Jesus Christ is right now as far as being led by the Spirit and walking a financial life that is in agreement with heaven's plans?

We hear, but we think it's coming from us or from someone else. We don't know the Lord that way yet, and the Word is not yet revealed to us.

When you know the Word, you know His creative power, because the Word you are called to know is the Word that spoke the world into existence! If I know God said it, why would I ever have second thoughts or doubts about what I heard?

81

Eli thought, "Wait a minute! Maybe the Lord is talking to Samuel. I remember when the Lord used to talk to me. Maybe the boy doesn't know that it is the Lord."

When the disciples saw Jesus walking on the water, they said, "It's a demon!" But Jesus said, "Fear not; it is I." Then Peter said, "If it's You, bid me to come to You on the water." The Word will work in your life when you really know it's God.

Most people read something off the pages of their Bible, and they don't know what to believe, because they don't know the Lord; neither is the Word of the Lord revealed to them yet. When the Word is revealed to you, you head in that direction, no matter what anyone says.

A Decision To Doubt

God wants to make wealthy Christians. God wants to make sufficient Christians. He wants to take care of every one of your needs and your wants. He wants to use you as a funnel through which He can channel His abundance.

Many things have not made their way into your life because of the way you think. Your lack of expectation keeps those miraculous additions of God out of your life by your subconscious decision to doubt.

So Eli said, "Maybe it's God talking to him. Boy, go back and lie down, and next time you hear the voice, say, 'Here am I, Lord.'" The boy returned to his room, and when he heard the voice again, he said, "Here am I, Lord." Then God revealed to Samuel the things that belonged to Samuel and his children.

Why didn't this sovereign God just reveal it to Samuel while he was thinking it was Eli? Why didn't He just say, "Stop, you dumb kid — it's not Eli, it's God, and I'm going to give you a revelation"? Because that's not the way God works.

I wonder how many times today you shrugged God off as if He were Eli? Then you blame Him for the results you get. You get Eli's results. Eli was fat, lazy, and couldn't even see.

The Lord is talking to you when you sense the Spirit of God moving on you. Sometimes certain phrases spoken by a preacher jump out at you and hit your spirit. What was said was a revealed thing that belongs to you.

God gave you exactly what He promised, a Word of God to reveal to you what His intentions are. You can say, "Here am I, Lord. I'm listening. What do You want me to do? Bring it on!"

Speaking Wisdom

Paul wrote in First Corinthians 2:

Howbeit we speak wisdom among them that are perfect [or mature]: yet not the wisdom of this world, nor of the princes of this world, that come to nought.

But we speak the wisdom of God in a mystery, even the hidden wisdom, which God ordained before the world unto our glory:

Which none of the princes of this world knew: for had they known it, they would not have crucified the Lord of glory.

1 Corinthians 2:7,8

How could the apostle Paul claim that he spoke wisdom among the mature, yet it was not the wisdom of this world or of the princes of this world, but the wisdom of God?

Why does the Church read this book and act like it doesn't have the wisdom of God? I'll tell you why: Whoever is reading this book and preaching it hasn't received the wisdom of the living Word in order to distribute it to the people. The Word of the Lord is precious.

When God speaks of His wisdom, He speaks of His ability to calculate how much water is in the ocean. He speaks of His ability to create. He speaks of the mind of the Lord. He speaks of how He spread heaven and how

He weighed the oceans in the palm of His hand, and He calls that His wisdom.

"We Have the Mind of Christ"

Paul quotes this concept in the New Testament, saying, "For who hath known the mind of the Lord, that he may instruct him? But we have the mind of Christ" (1 Corinthians 2:16).

Either we have the mind of Christ, or we don't. I choose to believe that Paul is telling the truth, and we do have the mind of Christ. And if we have the mind of Christ, we have His creative mind. We may have it in part, but the part we have is the part we know.

We have the mind of Christ — the same mind that created and put the universe in existence. That's God's wisdom, and God's wisdom is a creative wisdom.

Science is the *study* of what God has created. That's the wisdom of man. But the wisdom of God is *creating* it and putting it here. The wisdom of God made it.

How could you make something out of nothing? Wisdom! How could you speak a universe into existence? Wisdom! Why? Because the Word is alive. Wisdom! The Bible says we have that wisdom, and Paul said we speak that wisdom.

Someone will argue, "But we don't know what the Lord knows." We know part of it, so why don't we act on the part we know instead of concentrating on all the parts we *don't* know? If you will major on the one little part you've got, you will turn the world upside down for God.

The Glory in Creation

We are studying the silver, the gold, and the glory. The more I study, the more I find out that the glory is what *created* the gold and the silver.

Paul said, "We speak the wisdom of God in a mystery, even the hidden wisdom, which God ordained before the world unto our glory" (1 Corinthians 2:7).

God took His wisdom and shrouded it in a mystery — the same mystery that, had the princes of this world known, they would not have crucified the Lord of glory.

This is what God did: He ordained the hidden wisdom before the world unto *our* glory. Do you know, God didn't give Jesus at Calvary; God gave Jesus *before* He ever made man. God knew, "I'm going to make man in My image, after My likeness, but he's going to fall."

God knew it wouldn't be a goat, a sheep, or a pair of turtledoves that would buy man back. There was only one price that could possibly buy man back, and that was for God to give heaven's best, Christ Jesus — to give His own wisdom; to give Himself, the only wise God.

So before He ever created man, God had already assessed the price He would have to pay to reclaim man. If it was me, I would have changed my mind, but God ordained that wisdom in a mystery before the world was created, unto our glory. Before He ever made anything, He already knew the price He was going to have to pay.

God's Decision

His decision was, "I'm going to have to shroud wisdom in a mystery, send it down, and let it operate. And the wisdom of My Son is going to operate so miraculously and so supernaturally, the princes of the world will have no choice, for if they leave Him alone, everyone would believe on Him. They will be forced to try to do away with the influence of divine wisdom on planet Earth."

But by doing away with Christ, they actually enabled Him to return to glory, pour out the blood He paid for us on the mercy seat, and send the same wisdom back to Earth in the Person of the Holy Ghost to live in the lives of all who will receive Christ as Lord. The devil blew it royally 2000 years ago!

Do you know why the devil commissioned religion to preach against the supernatural, the divine, and that which comes from the wisdom of God? Because he is trying to keep back by fraud the things the wisdom of God will enable you to take from him, like you would take candy from a baby.

The Day God Bombed the Devil

The devil never caught God off guard. God already had a plan, and He had the "bomb" ready. And God dropped the bomb on the devil the day Christ was raised from the dead!

It was worse for the devil *after* Jesus was crucified than it was before. The devil is more threatened with Christ living in multiplied millions than when He lived in one body on Earth, because in those days, the devil was be able to evade Him. For example, if Jesus was ministering in Gadara, the devil could get away with things in Jerusalem.

But now the devil's got a problem: He's got to talk you out of the truth "Christ in you, the hope of glory." If he can't, suddenly the same wisdom and power of God is going to rise up inside you to claim what Jesus paid for 2000 years ago.

Praise God, such a formidible army is coming, there won't be a place on planet Earth where the devil can hide. This army will be made up of little children, teenagers, housewives, businessmen, preachers, and associates who are going to cast out devils, heal the sick, and perform miracles — and there is nothing the devil can do to stop them!

The Wisdom of God

We have been given the wisdom of God. Do you know why He's wise? Because He knows what is in the darkness, and the light dwells with Him. The reason He's wise is because He is the Spirit of wisdom and revelation. And that Spirit lives in you.

If you lack wisdom, you may ask of God, who gives liberally and doesn't hold back, and it will be given to you (James 1:5).

Wisdom for what? The wisdom of God is the kind of wisdom that advances you in every area of life. It is the wisdom that knows you shouldn't do something, even when it looks good; and it is the wisdom that says, "Go ahead and do that," even when everyone is discouraging you.

The Deep and Secret Things

...Eye hath not seen, nor ear heard, neither have entered into the heart of man, the things which God hath prepared for them that love him.

But God hath revealed them unto us by his Spirit: for the Spirit searcheth all things, yea, the deep things of God.

1 Corinthians 2:9,10

He revealeth the deep and secret things: he knoweth what is in the darkness, and the light dwelleth with him.

Daniel 2:22

How does God reveal the deep and secret things? *By His Spirit.* Why? *Because His Spirit searches all things; even the deep things of God.*

This means you must step beyond your own reasoning and understanding and follow the Spirit of God into His reasoning and understanding.

When you do, God will reveal to you things He has prepared for those who love him — things that haven't entered into the heart of man; things the natural eyes of man have not seen, their ears heard, or their eyes seen.

He reveals these things to us by His Spirit, because the Spirit does the searching. And if you follow Him, He will take you on a search, He will dig into the deep things of God, and He will reveal them to you. And when they are revealed to you, they belong to you — because the revealed things are yours.

When you start following God this closely, most people will think you're crazy, but you're following what the Bible says. If you run into believers who know the same God and follow the same Spirit, you will add to each other's knowledge.

You may find that others either don't know God or, if they're like Samuel, still think God is Eli. They haven't developed in their knowledge of the Word of God yet, and they need to understand that the Spirit of God is not a natural individual.

He leads us into the divine wisdom of God, and it is a mystery.

But you know what that mystery is: *Christ in you, the hope of glory!*

Chapter 5
Peace and Prosperity Come to the Temple

In my experience as a minister, I have found that one of the primary reasons why people do not serve God wholeheartedly — why they do not sell out to Jesus completely — is because they have their own agendas. They have certain needs, wants, and expectations for their lives, and they don't know if God will meet those needs or not.

I have learned that finances, careers, the future, and families are some of the reasons why most Christians do not sell out to God.

According to a reliable secular business magazine, between now and the year 2022, *the greatest transference of wealth in the free world is going to take place.* The magazine also said that the greatest percentage of this wealth will go to members of the Baby Boomer generation. Imagine, they didn't even know they were quoting me prophetically!

Even the world knows that there is going to be a great transference of wealth. This means that every greedy, money-hungry, self-seeking, self-promoting individual who hates God, loves himself, and is out to further his own kingdom or life and have more than everyone else so he can be more important than everyone else, will be going after that wealth.

But there is one element working for the child of God that cannot be bought, learned, or earned — and that is the supernatural element known as the favor, glory, or anointing of God. The anointing will see to it that the transference of wealth will end up in the right hands, not the wrong hands.

The next move of God will include financial prosperity and increase. Bear in mind, money is not evil. It's what one does with it that can be evil. Money can be good if it's in the right hands.

Building Whose Kingdom?

Some of my faith brethren have wondered why my wife and I work so hard and turn almost everything that comes in to the ministry back into the ministry, to the point of jeopardizing some of the personal goals the average successful human goes after.

People who have a shallow foundation on the Word of God and faith think that God gave the Word and faith so individuals could covet and have things. But God never speaks to *individuals* about the real purpose for the blessing — which is to build the kingdom of God. That is what we are working for.

So whenever we talk about the silver, the gold, and the glory, no one can accuse us of being materialistic, because that's not our objective. If we were seeking materialism, we wouldn't seek it at the hands of God.

Many have backslidden and gone into the world to get rich, because if a person is looking for a quick way to get rich, it's definitely not in obedience to the Spirit of God. *God is not into "get-rich-quick" schemes.*

If you prove yourself faithful in building the kingdom of God, God will put His favor on you, supplying all your needs and giving you more than you need. In the long run, you will find yourself better off financially than you could have planned for yourself.

The Nations Will Be Shaken

And I will shake all nations, and the desire of all nations shall come: and I will fill this house with glory, saith the Lord of hosts.

The silver is mine, and the gold is mine, saith the Lord of hosts.

The glory of this latter house shall be greater than of the former, saith the Lord of hosts: and in this place will I give peace, saith the Lord of hosts.

Haggai 2:7-9

This is an interesting portion of Scripture. At first glance, verse 7 may not make much sense, but the *Septuagint* translates it this way: "And I will convulse all nations, and the choice things of all nations will come, and I will fill this house with glory, says the Lord Almighty."

The *New English Bible* translates it, "And the treasures of all the nations will come in."

Verse 7 speaks of "the desire of all nations." Jesus said, "After all these things do the Gentiles seek. Don't you worry about what you're going to eat, what you're going to drink, how you're going to be dressed, or what kind of commodities you need in life, and fear, developing ulcers as a result and ending up competing with people, backstabbing people, lying, cheating, or compromising your Christian status in order to have things. Those are the desires of the heathen. The heathen seek or pursue those things."

There are people who are so educated they can't find a job. There are people who have done everything humanly possible to get ahead, but have not been successful. And there are people with a university education but no favor working for a person who has a sixth grade education and the favor of God.

After all these things the Gentiles seek. God is addressing a nation here — the nation of Israel. You can understand this prophetically; especially when you see a similar quote in Hebrews 12:26: "…Yet once more I shake not the earth only, but also heaven." This Scripture not only relates to the Old Testament; it is quoted here in the New Testament regarding the Church.

The Church As a Nation

You can also see that God was talking to us as if we were a nation. He was not saying, "Christian, I am going to build your kingdom"; He was addressing the Church, and He used the Church as one kind of nation and everyone else as different nations.

God said, "I am going to convulse the nations and their desires, their treasures or their most precious possessions, will come in." Jesus said, "Don't go after those things. That's what the heathen seek after." Instead, we are to desire the Lordship of Christ!

The first place I must go after the Lordship of Christ is in my heart.

The second place I must go after the Lordship of Christ is in my mind. I must seek His Lordship; I must pursue it in my thought life. I can't allow random thoughts to run through my mind. No, the Bible tells me to be transformed by *renewing* my own mind. Then, when my mind is renewed, it complies with the Lordship of Christ.

The third place I am supposed to pursue the Lordship of Christ is in my physical body. The Word tells me to offer my body as a living sacrifice, holy and acceptable unto God (Romans 12:1).

But my pursuit goes beyond that. I want the Lordship of Christ in my family, and I want the Lordship of Christ in you, your mind, your body, and your family.

Furthermore, I want the Lordship of Christ in my city, my state, my country, and throughout the Earth.

Why a Convulsing?

If that is our desire, God will convulse the nations. Let me tell you why there needs to be a convulsing. Poor people will give much more readily than the wealthy, yet there is enough wealth in the entire Earth to make everyone rich.

Why isn't everyone rich? Because the wealth of the Earth is hoarded. The Bible speaks of vaults and hoarded wealth kept by a spirit of greed and control. The devil knows if wealth gets into the right hands, it will be used for the right purposes — and the devil can't afford a well-funded Gospel!

The shaking is coming because the grip of the heathen over their treasures is slipping. Between now and the year 2022, a lot of slipping is going to take place. The heathen are convulsing and being shaken, and their grip is being loosened.

The thing they desire the most — the wealth of the Earth — is coming to a people who haven't even made it a priority, because their priority and desire is to build God's kingdom. Christians see a glorified Christ. We see a healthy army preaching the Gospel to every nation. We don't know how God is going to fund it, but we know He will. And while we are going after the things of God, here comes the desire of the nations!

We are soldiers in the army of the Lord. There is a giant with our name on his forehead. Only we can kill that giant.

God's Glory in the Temple

God is going to shake the nations, and He is going to fill His house with glory. He was not really referring to Solomon's Temple or the Temple Zerubbabel built with Herod; He was not referring to any earthly temple. He was going beyond that, speaking about a spiritual temple, the temple of God, which is made up of "lively stones" — members of the Body of Christ.

Then in Haggai 2:8, God said, "The silver is mine, and the gold is mine." Why would He flood the resources of the nations into His temple unless He intended to use those resources to take over?

God said in the next verse, "The glory of this latter house shall be greater than of the former, saith the Lord of hosts: And in this place will I give peace...." This can't apply to anything but the Church. You never have peace until you get in it, and you can't get in it until you know the Prince of Peace.

According to the *New English Bible,* verse 9 is translated, "This place will I grant prosperity and peace. This is the very word of the Lord of hosts." *The Amplified Bible* renders it, "And in this place I will give peace and prosperity, says the Lord."

Christian authors have actually written books *against* prosperity. If you write a book against prosperity, give the book away!

Preoccupied With Poverty

Why does God want you taken care of? Show me a witnessing Christian who is losing his house, his marriage is breaking apart because of money problems, and his life is falling apart because of money problems. You can't show me such a person. The breed doesn't exist.

That's why we have seen a halt in revival. The devil, through religion, has sold the Church a bunch of lies and gotten Christians so preoccupied with their own poverty, they have been afraid to venture into the prosperity of the Lord.

A double minded man is unstable in all of his ways. The Bible says in James 1:7 that a person like that cannot receive anything from the Lord.

We've thought that a double minded man is the man who says and believes something and then changes his mind about it. A definition of double mindedness includes that, but that's not the real definition of a double minded man. Changing your mind is not being double minded!

Receiving the Will of God

Actually, double mindedness is believing one thing in your *conscious* mind and believing something completely different in your *subconscious* mind or your heart.

Being double minded is saying yes intellectually, but on the inside there is absolutely no agreement with that, because you can't see it happening.

The Bible tells us to guard our hearts with all diligence. Why? Because religion tries to sow negative seeds or thoughts via religion, doctrines, the world, and traditions of men. These seeds try to lodge in your heart and bear fruit contrary to the plan of God.

All of us probably have certain thoughts or ways of perceiving God in our hearts that limit us in receiving the will of God perfectly in our lives.

Measuring Wealth

The world teaches us that wealth equates to money, but we have discovered that wealth cannot always be measured solely in terms of money. *Wealth is anything of value that God can bring into your life to get a job accomplished.*

For example, a woman with an arm broken in four places came to our church. Her doctor told her, "You'll be out of work for 18 months."

We were having a revival. The power of God healed her arm instantly. She came up on the platform the next day to testify that she was totally healed. She could move her arm!

Her healing was worth tens of thousands of dollars to her. That's wealth! God redeemed her from the curse of being unemployed for 18 months.

A member of our church was offered all the old equipment from a workout gym that was getting new equipment. They gave all their old equipment to him, and he stored it in a warehouse. The old equipment was in perfect condition.

He recently called me to ask, "Could you use the gym equipment in your new building?"

"What do you have?" I asked.

"I've got *everything*," he said.

If we were to go out and buy all the equipment needed to furnish a gym, we might have to spend $100,000. That's wealth!

Now we can have a Christian gym where people won't have to mingle with the heathen, listen to their stinking music, or be exposed to their ungodly behavior.

Our Christian gym can also act as a "net," because an unsaved person who may not want to attend church may agree to come to the gym. Little does he know that when he comes to the gym, he might end up on the floor, praying in other tongues as the Spirit gives him utterance!

Peace and Prosperity in the Temple

God is going to give peace and prosperity to His people. Where? In the Temple of the Lord — the one that is the latter house — the Church.

How is He going to do it? There's a whole lot of shaking that will be going on; and the grip of those who are hoarding wealth and keeping it in the camp of evil is being loosed. They are not going to be able to hang on to it for much longer. A great deal of distribution will take place for the sake of the Church.

Don't pray for God to do something for you. If you seek wealth for yourself, you will remove yourself from God's way of prosperity.

Instead, pray that a spirit of giving continues to inspire the Church. If there is a spirit of giving in the Church, some of the benefits will spill over into your life. Or pray that God will bless you financially so you can bless the Church.

While the world is frantically caught up in the rat race, chasing their desires, those desires will slip through their hands and come to people who are seeking the kingdom.

Millions are working hard but are worried about their wealth. What they are toiling for, you will receive. This principle is found throughout the Bible; it's not something new.

How the Jews Plundered the Egyptians

Everything the children of Israel asked the Egyptians for, the Egyptians gave them.

"Can I have that bracelet?"

"Yes."

"And those rings over there? How about that emerald? The furniture? The clothing?"

Everything they asked for, they got. The Bible says that's how they *plundered* Egypt. The Egyptians didn't even come to their senses until the Jews were already at the Red Sea.

They would have made it to the Promised Land with all this treasure if they hadn't decided to make something with it. Their golden calf became their god.

What's on Your Wish List?

If God were to show up someday at your house and ask, "What would you have Me do for you?" you would exclaim, "Wait, wait, Lord! I've got a list here somewhere!" People have their lists, and they go through those lists asking God for many things. What do you pray for?

God showed up one night and said to King Solomon, "Ask what I shall give thee" (2 Chronicles 1:7). Notice Solomon's wise reply:

> And Solomon said unto God, Thou hast shewed great mercy unto David my father, and hast made me to reign in his stead.
>
> Now, O Lord God, let thy promise unto David my father be established: for thou hast made me king over a people like the dust of the earth in multitude.
>
> Give me now wisdom and knowledge, that I may go out and come in before this people: for who can judge this thy people, that is so great?
>
> 2 Chronicles 1:8-10

Did you notice that what Solomon asked for was not for himself? This means that just by adjusting your attitude, you can benefit your life. Solomon sought God's will. He wanted to judge his people fairly. He wanted wisdom and knowledge so he could be a blessing to them. That's awesome!

James said, "If any of you lack wisdom, let him ask of God, that giveth to all men liberally, and upbraideth not; and it shall be given him" (James 1:5).

Ask for Wisdom

The reason why some Christians don't have resources is because, instead of asking for wisdom, they ask for resources. Wisdom is directly linked to your purpose.

Let me give you an example. How many people say, "When I grow up, I want to buy a car to live in"? Why don't they say this? Because a car isn't meant to be a house. You can live in one, but your stay won't last long. The manufacturer designed that automobile for a different purpose.

You were created for a specific purpose, too. Your purpose is to do God's will. The moment you say, "God, I want wisdom to fulfill my purpose," every resource attached to your purpose will start coming your way! God said He will shake the nations; He didn't say you will go out and get the desire of the nations. He said the desire of the nations will come.

Does that mean we don't have to work? That would be ridiculous! Does that mean we don't cast the net in faith? No, it just means that the method by which we increase is supernatural.

Fulfilling God's Purpose

You can't explain why the favor of God is blessing you, but you know why. Why? Because all you want to do is your purpose. If your purpose is to do whatever God's will is, the resources attached to fulfilling it will automatically start to flow your way.

Yes, you have a purpose in life, and your purpose is *fruitfulness.* If part of your purpose is to be the priest of your home, all the resources necessary for that role will flow your way. Beyond that, your purpose may include your role in the church, the world, and so forth.

Solomon asked God for wisdom to fulfill his purpose, and God was pleased with his request. This was God's reply.

> **And God said to Solomon, Because this was in thine heart, and thou hast not asked riches, wealth, or honour, nor the life of thine enemies, neither yet hast asked long life; but hast asked wisdom and knowledge for thyself, that thou mayest judge my people, over whom I have made thee king:**
>
> **Wisdom and knowledge is granted unto thee; and I will give thee riches, and wealth, and honour, such as none of the kings have had that have been before thee, neither shall there any after thee have the like.**
>
> **2 Chronicles 1:11,12**

God was saying, "You didn't seek things for yourself. I am going to give you wisdom and knowledge. Because you wanted it for My people, everything associated with expressing that wisdom on a large scale is granted to you, and I will also give you riches, wealth, and honor." I love that word "riches"!

Solomon and "the Greater One"

Solomon was universally recognized for his wisdom. Jesus said people came from everywhere to hear the wisdom of Solomon. This included the Queen of Sheba, who was dazzled by Solomon. But today One much greater than Solomon is available to us. Christ is much wiser and richer than Solomon!

Why hasn't the reputation of the Greater One become so universal that every knee has bowed and every tongue confessed His Lordship? It's because while we have embraced Christ fully, the devil has separated us from expecting the wisdom, the knowledge, and the resources necessary to globally share the Gospel. That is all about to change!

If Solomon's wealth and riches came from the people he reigned over, why wasn't his father, King David, as rich as he was; why wasn't King Saul, Israel's first king, as rich as he was; and why weren't the kings who followed him equally as rich?

Where did the resources come from that made this king one of the wealthiest — if not the wealthiest — person on planet Earth? Why would God do this for Solomon?

God explained, "Because Solomon's main desire was to have the wisdom and the knowledge to deal properly with his people, I am going to give him every penny necessary to express that on a universal scale." That's awesome!

The Riches of Solomon

So Solomon became the richest man on Earth. The Temple or house he built for the Lord cost $174 billion. Talk about a building project! That's $174 *billion!*

God had promised, "...I will fill this house with glory ...The silver is mine, and the gold is mine, and..in this place will I give him peace..." (Haggai 2:7-9).

I don't know how many people Solomon had working for him, but his food bill alone was $17,400 a day. His many wives ate a lot, too. But Solomon wasn't worried about putting food on the table. His personal offering at the time the Temple was dedicated was nearly $10 million.

In one year alone, Solomon was given $20 million worth of gold. When people came to see and hear the wisdom of Solomon, they brought valuable and exotic gifts to him.

The Worth of Lively Stones

If the house Solomon built for the Lord was valued at $174 billion, I wonder what each stone was worth? In other words, if the *corporate whole* has a certain value, the *individual* lively stone, the individual believer, also has a certain value.

I am trying to show you that God's economy for the last days is not going to be random. God is not going to say, "This one is rich, and this one is poor." That's ridiculous!

If we're all involved in the same purpose, and if we are all supposed to be contributing to the same cause, it's God's responsibility to see to it that our personal resources come. I didn't say it; the Word of God says it!

I don't want to be anything other than what God called me to be. God called me to raise up His people, bless them, teach them, and help them to become an influence on planet Earth. And do you know what He gave me? Baby Boomers. God gave me mostly Boomers.

The day will come when someone in our church will say, "I'll give $1 million to that," and others will say, "I'll give $100,000 to that." The amounts will vary, but it won't matter. What matters is the fact that it is the will of God to fulfill the purpose of this house — the latter house of the Church.

Jesus told us that the lily is dressed better than Solomon was in all his glory. You're worth more than the lily, so a Christian should be dressed better than Solomon.

Was Jesus Poor?

The soldiers at the Crucifixion rolled dice to win possession of Jesus' fabulous robe. It was seamless, woven from the top to the bottom. You couldn't afford a robe like that today, yet some Christians are so convinced that Jesus was poor.

He was born in a manger and wrapped in swaddling clothes. Meanwhile, before He was even born, a star appeared in the East, and three wise men recognized that someone wiser and greater was being born in a far-off land.

The wise men acted on the revelation and left their own country to follow the star. That's the difference between a wise person and a miserably informed person. The wise person is not simply a hearer; he or she acts on the revelation.

The wise men arrived in time to give gifts to the young child. This was a move of God in its infancy. It hasn't done a miracle yet. It doesn't have a budget. It hasn't reached the world yet — but it deserves some resources.

The wise men walked in bearing gold. Do you think they gave Jesus a little gold chain? That's what I don't understand about religious people. Where do they get their thinking? What version of the Bible are they reading?

Appropriate Gifts

What kind of gold did wise men, kings, or ambassadors bring from afar as an appropriate gift for a king?

What if ambassadors told a king, "We thought we'd pick up this little chain for you. Turn around, and we'll put it on you." The king would respond, "Behead them!" No, ambassadors brought treasure chests full of gold to kings. And no doubt, the wise men brought lavish amounts of gold, frankincense, and myrrh to Jesus.

We like to spiritualize the purpose for those gifts, but we can't get away from the fact or the reality that they were precious, valuable gifts. That was why the angel of the Lord could show up and tell Joseph, "Take the mother and child and go to Egypt, because Herod is going to seek to kill Him."

Joseph, Mary, and Jesus went to Egypt and lived there until the Lord recalled them to their own country. They had no problem with finances. They lived off the gold, the frankincense, and the myrrh. "Poor" Jesus traveled in style to and from Egypt!

There's a "Baby" in You

By the same token, this is what happens to people who get born again. The Bible says that when you are born again, Christ is formed in you. There's a "baby" in you. Your new nature is Christlike but, as a child, you should desire the sincere milk of the Word so you might grow (1 Peter 2:2).

There are those like Herod who will seek to kill that "baby" before it comes to maturity. It's possible, because the Judaizers did it to the Galatians, and Paul wrote, "I am travailing again, as if I were a woman giving birth to a child, so that Christ would be formed in you" (Galatians 4:19 paraphrased). Why? Because "religion" had killed the Christ-nature in the new converts by getting them out of grace and into works.

New converts lose their connection with Christ, back-slide, and return to their ungodly lifestyles because they don't understand that the moment the "baby" is born in them, gold, frankincense, and myrrh are on the way to them.

God will take care of them so they can take care of the vision until the vision grows up to accomplish the purpose that God has set forth in them!

Chapter 6
Faith, Confession, and the Promises of God

Now the Lord had said unto Abram, Get thee out of thy country, and from thy kindred, and from thy father's house, unto a land that I will shew thee.

Genesis 12:1

Would you like to be as close to God as you can get? I believe each one of us has been granted the privilege and the invitation to draw near to God.

The way we draw near to Him is through our *thoughts.* Our thoughts either separate us from God or draw us to Him. When I read a Scripture, I meditate upon it. What I think about it determines what I do with it.

James wrote, "Be ye doers of the word, and not hearers only, deceiving your own selves" (James 1:23). When you hear the Word, and it doesn't change your thoughts or affect your decisions, you are deceiving yourself.

Working in the Glory

Whenever we speak of the glory, we are speaking about God's plan for the last of the last days. The glory of God will be revealed. It will cover the Earth, and it will manifest in the most powerful revival the world has ever seen!

And you and I have been given the invitation to draw near to God with our thoughts, our will, our spirit, and our agreement — because the closer we draw to God, the greater God can use us in His plan for the last days! However, if you limit God in your life, you can't limit God in my life. My decisions affect my life.

Most of us were raised either with a religious background or with some religious concepts. After we are born again and get involved in a church, we approach God with the same misconceptions we were taught by "religion" and the world itself.

We approach God as if we have left neither our former "country" nor our "kindred." We try to fit God into our family, our culture, our background, our education, and our limitations. We try to keep Him in a little box in our lives. We try to incorporate Him into a set of possessions like we would a new suit or a new car.

God's Call

But God didn't call Himself into our country; He called us *out* of our country just like He called Abraham out of his. Furthermore, He didn't call Himself into our kindred; He called us *out* of our kindred. And the way He called Abraham is the way He called you and me.

There is a reason why God calls you out. He calls you *out* so He can call you *in*.

He called the children of Israel out of Egypt to call them into the Promised Land.

He calls you out of the world to call you into His kingdom.

He calls you out of your kindred to call you into His kindred.

He calls you out of your country to call you into His country.

He calls you out of your family to call you into His family.

The Laws of the Kingdom

I cannot become a citizen of a new nation unless I understand the laws of that nation. Otherwise, I would be trying to obtain citizenship while I'm an outlaw.

In this nation, we don't grant citizenship to outlaws, criminals, or convicted felons. To qualify as a citizen of this nation, you must be law-abiding.

Did you know that God has laws in His kingdom, and there is a culture in His kingdom? Culture is nothing more than a mind-set. But some people might say, "You don't understand my family tree." No, you don't understand the truth! After you are born again, you are hooked up to God's family tree, and you develop a different mind-set.

So when we discuss the glory, we are discussing what God does through His people.

The Key To Coming Out of Your Country

Hebrews 11 provides the key to coming out of your country and never going back. It says if the heroes of faith had been mindful of the country they had come out of, they would have had opportunity to return. The point is, don't be mindful of what you came out of. Come out of it, and keep on coming out of it!

I have no desire to turn back, and I'm not even referring to sin; I'm referring to religion. I'm referring to folly. I'm referring to believing what I want to believe about the Word of God rather than what the Word of God actually says.

The keys to this final revival, as we found in our previous studies, are: first, the anointing or the power of God to do the job; second, the finances and the resources to do the job.

Let me show you how it works. It makes no sense for you to have a blessed pastor and not be blessed in your own life. It's just like it doesn't make sense to be born into a rich family and live poverty-stricken for the rest of your life.

It's important to understand how God operates. The vast majority of Christians on planet Earth are sitting in churches they worked hard to build. The only reason they won't get out of that "country" and move to a place where there's green grass and where they can be fed, nourished, and taught in the ways of the Lord is because where their treasure is, their heart is also. They put all of their efforts into building that church, and now they won't vacate and move on. They need to get out of their familiar territory.

Leaving the Past Behind

Let's go beyond that. Some people work in a company they don't like, for a boss they can't stand, because they've been working there too long to leave and move on.

In this final hour, we'd better understand these two things: (1) our purpose for living and (2) God's ability to fulfill our purpose.

Our purpose for living is to change the world for Jesus and to change others!

His ability to do it through us demands several things. For example, He needs to keep us healthy so we won't die before our purpose has been fulfilled. God keeps us healthy if we know how to draw on His promises for good health.

Abraham couldn't be mindful of his old country, where idolatry and heathenism were entrenched. He had to go out like a sojourner, a traveler. God blessed him along the way. The Bible speaks of the blessing of Abraham in Galatians 3:14: "That the blessing of Abraham might come on the Gentiles through Jesus Christ...."

So God has a blessing He will place on our lives. That blessing is not money, healing, or health. Those things come as a result of the blessing. When you get the blessing, it's an all-inclusive package.

Exploring the Whole House

We all know it would be foolish to buy a house and live only in the bedroom. There are other rooms in that house. If visitors came and said, "Show us your house," would you show them only the bedroom? When they asked, "What else have you got," would you say, "I don't know; I never go out of this room"?

Some Christians have never explored beyond their salvation. They're living in a big house, but they've never seen anything except the room of the salvation of the soul!

They won't step into the rooms of financial increase, abundance, and prosperity. They won't step into the room of activity and blessing in God. They won't step into the room of healing or divine health. They live beneath their privileges. They're limited to one aspect of God's provision.

Ephesians 2:6 tells us we inherited the throne of glory when Christ was raised from the dead, because He raised us up together with Him and made us to sit together with Him in heavenly places. That's when heaven was opened to us, and the throne of glory was made accessible to us.

Coming Boldly to the Throne

And the Bible doesn't suggest it; it *commands* us in Hebrews 4:16 to come *boldly* to the throne of grace to obtain mercy and find grace *in time of need.*

That means whenever we have a need, we have the commandment to approach the throne with boldness. But how are we to approach the throne if we don't think it's accessible? Where will boldness come from if our feelings are contrary to our position; if we feel that God is a thousand miles away; and if we wonder if He will hear us?

Our prayers won't work unless we know beyond a shadow of a doubt that He promised us accessibility to the throne and commanded us to come boldly with our needs. We've got to know God is listening when we call forth His promises. We've got to know He will back up those promises.

After some Christians acquire a little understanding of the message of faith and confession, they immediately throw it down and shy away from it, because they don't understand why it is the way it is.

God Describes Himself

Let me tell you why it is the way it is. In the Old Testament, God gave compound names to describe Himself.

"Who are You?" men asked Him.

"I am Jehovah God," He said. That's His name.

"What does His name mean?" men wondered. It means, "I am *Jehovah-Shammah.* I am present. I am victory." Those names God gave identified Himself.

"Which God do you serve?" I serve the God of the Lord Jesus Christ. I serve Jehovah.

Some might say, "Buddha and Jehovah are the same." No, Buddha is Buddha, and Jehovah is Jehovah. It's not "Jebuddha." *It's what God said about Himself that matters.*

He is the God that healeth thee, *Jehovah-Rapha.* He is *Jehovah-Jireh*, your Provider. That's His name.

Religion said, "Yes, but He's God — and God can do anything He wants to." By this they mean that even though He is the Compassionate One who heals you, He can also keep you sick to teach you something. But to believe that, you've got to make the Word of God a lie!

God said He has magnified His Word above His name (Psalm 138:2). If He asks people, "Who am I?" the people will respond, "God." Then He will say, "Don't be too impressed by that. I, God, can do anything, and I have magnified My Word above My name so you would not dare accuse Me of lying."

Therefore if God says, "Believe on the Lord Jesus Christ, and thou shalt be saved," and I reply, "I tried that, but it doesn't work," the only one lying is me.

Rightly Handling the Word

I can't say, "I tried to be saved, but God doesn't want to save me." I can't say, "God saves those who are predestined to be saved." I can't mess around with the Word of God without trying to make God — who cannot lie — a liar. Who, then, is responsible with rightly handling the word of truth? I am.

Can you honestly say you have read through the Bible, from Genesis to Revelation, more than three times?

Few people have. Yet if I were to ask how many have an opinion, everyone would say they had one. Read the Word of God.

The Bible warns about not having many teachers, because teachers will receive a greater condemnation. In other words, before we are teachers and have opinions, let's dig deep enough and far enough and maintain the attitude, "Even though that's my present position, if I dig into the Word of God and find out I'm wrong, I will change what I believe."

As you get into the Word of God, you will read, "I am God. I make evil and make good; I make rich and make poor" (Isaiah 45:7). And you will read this verse in First Samuel 2:8:

He raiseth up the poor out of the dust, and lifteth up the beggar from the dunghill, to set them among princes, and to make them inherit the throne of glory: for the pillars of the earth are the Lord's, and he hath set the world upon them.

People read this and say, "Aha! Do you see that? God is in charge of everything, and He can do anything He wants to." What they need to understand is that "...the prophecy came not in old time by the will of man: but holy men of God spake as they were moved by the Holy Ghost," according to Second Peter 1:21.

Progressive Revelation

Do you realize that Moses didn't have all the truth, and Isaiah didn't have all the truth? As a matter of fact, they prophesied only *a portion* of the truth, being ignorant of the rest of the truth. Why? Because neither of them was "a walking Bible." Only Christ was the complete Word.

In order for you to get the full picture, you can't take a piece of the puzzle and say, "This is the full picture." You've got to see the full picture and say, "This is the full picture."

The Bible is *progressive revelation,* and although you are only responsible for what you know, you are also responsible for what is available to you — what is right under your nose; what you have access to.

In light of that, look at Deuteronomy 30:19: "I call heaven and earth to record this day against you, that I have set before you life and death, blessing and cursing: therefore choose life, that both thou and thy seed may live."

Notice God separates life and blessing into one side and death and cursing into another side. You can't split a miracle, as Eastern religions do, into *yin* and *yang*, and call it one. Yet in the Church, we have drawn a circle, made it *yin* and *yang*, and said, "God does both good and evil. He does whatever He wants to, because He's God — but He's still good."

The Devil: An Outlaw

No, God is not a Buddhist. He doesn't fill both sides of the circle as both good and evil. Neither is the devil on God's payroll. The devil doesn't do evil so good will come out of it. The devil is an outlaw, and God is able to turn what he does into good — but He never sanctions or authorizes the devil to do evil. *Everything the devil does, he does as an outlaw.* Otherwise, God would not have given us authority over all the power of the devil. If we are authorized to put the enemy in check, God must want him in check!

The Bible calls the devil a thief. You know how a thief operates — in the dark. When you turn on the light, the thief runs.

Do you know why the devil is against the message of prosperity? It's because "The entrance of thy words giveth light…" (Psalm 119:130), and when light comes, the devil is out of a job in your life. The devil doesn't want to stop stealing, because when a thief is caught, he has to repay you seven times, according to the Word.

The devil wants to keep doing what he does. Jesus said, "The thief cometh not, but for to steal, and to kill, and to destroy: I am come that they might have life, and that they might have it more abundantly" (John 10:10).

We Are God's Representatives

Jesus rebuked a storm. Did God *send* the storm? No. Did God *allow* the storm? Yes. God allows anything that His representatives won't take authority over.

God turned His authority over to His representatives on planet Earth and told them, "...whatsoever thou shalt bind on earth shall be bound in heaven: and whatever thou shalt loose on earth shall be loosed in heaven" (Matthew 16:19).

We're God's representatives on Earth. That's why He sent the Holy Ghost: The Holy Ghost works in agreement with God's Word to bring to pass His power on Earth.

For us to understand this, we must carefully study the whole Bible; we can't casually read through the Bible once and have an opinion without digging in.

Notice in Deuteronomy 30:19 that God put both life and death and blessing and cursing before us. In other words, He said, "Think about it and choose."

You can't respond, "Well, I don't know. I'll take anything." God not only told you what's ahead of you; He has commanded you to choose.

If you're an obedient Christian, all you need to do is look at Deuteronomy 30:11: "For this commandment which I commanded thee this day, it is not hidden from thee, neither is it far off."

This is not a *suggestion*. People who refuse to choose and blame it on God's sovereignty are living a life of disobedience, because He never told you to choose anything you want, did He? He didn't say you could choose anything you want. He tells you to choose life.

The chances are, if you choose death and cursing with your thoughts and your confidence, three things will happen to you: (1) You will experience death; (2) you will experience cursing; and (3) you will experience judgment — because you were guilty of choosing what God told you *not* to choose.

Receiving the Blessing of Abraham

Choose life! How do you do this? Life can't flow without choosing Christ, the Author of life. So you must choose Christ as your Savior. Then, the Bible tells us, the blessing of Abraham comes on you through Jesus Christ, and you receive the promise of the Spirit through faith.

The Hebrew word for "blessing" throughout the Old Testament means divine goodwill or grace. Blessing is happiness, health, long life, increase, and peace among men. It results in your prosperity and wealth.

When you study, you find that when God said, "Choose life and choose blessing," He was saying, "Choose peace, long life, prosperity, wealth, and health among humanity."

But what if you don't know how to resist the devil when he comes to steal what God gave you? What if you don't know you've got the right to resist him? How are you going to say no to him if you think he might be on assignment from heaven? How are you going to stand in your authority wearing the whole armor of God if you're not sure who sent that messenger or who sanctioned the assignment?

Do You Know Your Rights?

You can't do it. And if you can't, how can God hold you accountable for something you can never do? That would mean He's unreasonable. It would mean He's given you a commandment you can never fulfill, because He can't tell you to choose blessing if the choice is not yours.

If you're a preacher and you choose life, think how many more sermons you will have preached by the time you're 85 than if you had died at age 40.

If you don't know your rights, you may die before your time. Then, when you get to heaven, God will say, "You're too early; what are *you* doing here?"

You'll say, "I don't know. It's your fault. I chose life and blessing, but it just didn't work." But God never asks you anything unreasonable. He never asks you to do something you can't do.

Has anyone resisted the devil and failed? Certainly. Why? Because authority doesn't work when you're living in disobedience.

You can't live in sin and stand up and rebuke the devil. You can't rob God in your tithes and offerings and say it doesn't work. Your confession can't consist of complaining, griping, and gossiping and then expect to be victorious in confrontations with the adversary.

If you are to choose life, you must choose it with your thoughts. You can't be mindful of the "old country." You choose life with your words. You choose it with your actions.

The Greatest Battle

When alternative thoughts badger you — "Your mother had arthritis…your grandmother was crippled in a wheelchair because of arthritis…what if you get arthritis?" — you've got to say, "Wait a minute! I've chosen something else."

"What if what you chose doesn't happen?"

This is the greatest battle for most people. They battle with the fear that what they choose won't happen. That would make God a liar, wouldn't it? What a terrible thing!

But it's impossible for God to be a liar! If your choice to live is not working, it means you're doing something wrong. God is not a liar. He can't lie. He is God, and He has magnified His Word above His name. In other words, He is bound to what He said 100 percent of the time!

Notice God promises life and blessing for you and your seed. If your teach your children to choose life and God's blessing from the time they're little, they won't know anything else.

Personal Responsibility

As we saw in First Samuel 2:8, the reason God raises the poor out of the dunghill is to set them among princes and cause them to inherit the throne of glory.

The verses before that say, "The Lord killeth, and maketh alive: he bringeth down to the grave, and bringeth up. The Lord maketh poor, and maketh rich: he bringeth low, and lifteth up" (1 Samuel 2:6,7).

The religious person hears that and says, "See, I told you so!" But you've got to put that together with Deuteronomy 30:19. You will find that someone chose death.

So it's not really *God* who kills; it's the decision *the person* made. God presented him with two alternatives. He said, "Son, if you choose this way, this will happen; and if you choose the alternative, son, this will happen."

It would be like my giving you these two alternatives. I could say, "There's an elevator behind the first door, but the second door does not lead to an elevator. If you go through the first door, you'll end up in the elevator. If you go through the second door, you'll fall down six stories and break your bones!"

That's just the way it is. You would be foolish to choose the wrong door. And you can't choose the wrong door and come back and blame me. Ultimately, God is the only One who can say, "I told you so." The laws of the kingdom of God work all the time.

Our God Is Reliable

We once lived in a beautiful house that was 100 years old. We renovated it, but the electrical wiring was like some people's prayer life: It only worked some of the time. When these people pray, it's like pulling the cord on an unreliable light socket.

They say, "O God, we believe. But is He going to answer my prayer? I don't know, but I'm believing..."

God is not unreliable like the electrical wiring in our old house. One morning I went into my closet, pulled the cord, and two seconds later the light bulb decided to come on. I never knew when it was going to come on. Sometimes it worked, and sometimes it didn't. And sometimes the bulb just blew out.

But our God is not like that. He's never been like that with me. Everything He has ever said to me is not only the truth, but it works. And whenever it seems as if it's not working, I find that the problem is at my end, not His. God is not a man that He should lie (Numbers 23:19). You can put stock in what He says!

> **That their hearts might be comforted, being knit together in love, and unto all riches of the full assurance of understanding, to the acknowledgement of the mystery of God, and of the Father, and of Christ;**
>
> **In whom are hid all the treasures of wisdom and knowledge.**
>
> **Colossians 2:2,3**

Many of us read Paul's epistles and jump right over verses like verse 2, wondering, "What in the world is he talking about?" But we must remember that everything in the Bible is there for a reason.

When verse 2 says, "That their hearts might be comforted," do you believe God wants your heart to be comforted? How can you be comforted if you're not sure?

The next phrase is, "being knit together in love." Here we have the Church's heart knit together by the Holy Ghost, united in the bond or the spirit of love, "unto all riches of the full assurance of understanding."

Riches or Poverty?

Riches in the Bible are anything you have in abundance. Looking at this in context, you find this is an abundance of assurance of understanding. That means you are to be sure that you understand. How much assurance do you have? You have an abundance of assurance and understanding.

If you allow doubt to enter your mind and say, "I wonder if I really believe the Word? I wonder if Brother So-and-so is right, or if Brother Such-and-such is right?" you allow *the riches* of assurance of understanding to depart. You are left with a *poverty* or deficit of assurance.

Religion asks, "Are you sure?" In religion's opinion, it looks like one day it's going to be fixed, but right now it's broken.

Verse 2 continues, "to the acknowledgement of the mystery of God." Paul wants us to acknowledge the mystery of God.

What's the Mystery?

What is the mystery of God? *Christ in you, the hope of glory!* Colossians 1:27 says, "...the riches of the glory of this mystery among the Gentiles; which is Christ in you, the hope of glory."

This means that when the Holy Ghost moved in, Christ moved in! That's what God calls the mystery.

Here Paul tells you to acknowledge the fact that Christ lives in you. Why? Because verse 3 tells you, "In whom are hid all *the treasures of wisdom and knowledge.*"

Can you have wisdom for a revival? Can you have knowledge for a move of God? How does wisdom come? Wisdom comes in the form of ideas — divine ideas. Understanding comes in the form of divine ideas. You can have wisdom with natural things, but did you know that you can have wisdom with spiritual things as well?

How many of you have looked at a verse you've read a thousand times, and all of a sudden you exclaimed, "I just saw that for the first time!" That wisdom and understanding is already in Christ, and Christ is where? In you.

Why? So you can draw on the wisdom and the understanding that is already in you. It's not in your brain, and it's not in your ability. It's not because you earned it; it's because He's in you, and He loves you. It's not because

Dr. Christian Harfouche

Cathedral of Praise in Manila, Philippines. Pastored by Dr. David Sumrall, nephew of Lester Sumrall. *(Above)*

Dr. Lester Sumrall with Pastor Robin and Dr. Christian Harfouche. *(Below)*

International Miracle Institute's Founding Class.

International Miracle Institute students receive their second year achievement in studies.

International Miracle Institute's Founding Class receives their three year diploma in ministerial studies. (Above)

Dr. Lester Sumrall ministering to an International Miracle Institute's first graduating class.. (Below)

Dr. Lester Sumrall worshipping the Lord with Dr. Christian and Pastor Robin Harfouche at the graduation. (Above)

Totally deaf man TOTALLY healed in Hawaii. (Below)

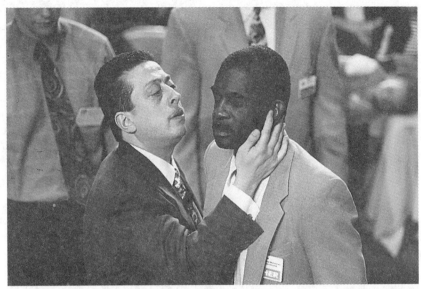

Dr. Harfouche checks this man's restored hearing. (Above)

This South African baby was born deaf but heard for the first time after Dr. Harfouche prayed for the child. (Below)

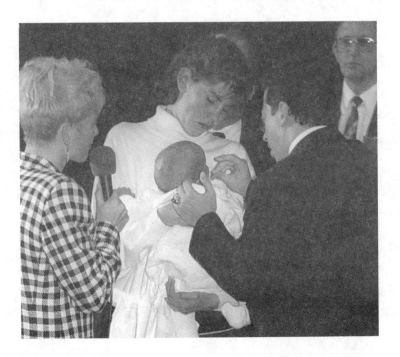

Pastor Robin ministering words of knowledge to a South African congregation. (Above)

Pastor Robin Harfouche leading Praise and Worship at the Tampa Sun Dome. (Below)

Dr. Harfouche teaching at the Tampa Sun Dome.

Dr. Harfouche ministering to an expectant New England Crusade crowd.

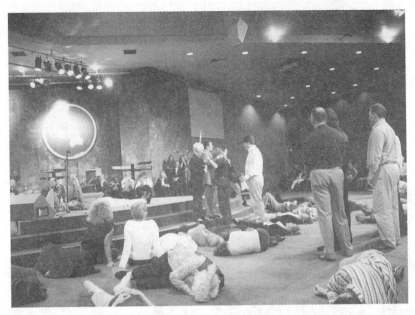

Dr. Harfouche and Pastor Robin Harfouche ministering healing in Australia.

Dr. Harfouche raises leg braces removed for the first time in years after a Bangor, Maine crusade.

Tampa Campmeeting 1998

Dr. Christian and Pastor Robin Harfouche ministering in Lagos, Nigeria. (Above)

100's saved at an Indian crusade. (Below)

*South African Woman running immediately after being healed from
paralysis and confinement to a wheel chair. (Above)*
Dr. Harfouche is preparing to preach to an Australian crowd. (Below)

Dr. Harfouche adds these crutches to a collection of no longer needed medical aids.

Total hearing restored after Dr. Harfouche laid hands on this gentleman.

Manila, Philippines

Pastor Robin leads this Australian congregation into the Realms of Glory.

you're worthy; it's because He's in there, and you can draw from His wisdom.

If You Lack Wisdom

We've read where James said if anyone lacks wisdom, he may ask God, who gives liberally to everyone and doesn't upbraid, and wisdom shall be given to him (James 1:5). How does that wisdom come?

You ask for wisdom, and then you acknowledge the mystery. You say, "I know I don't have the wisdom or the understanding of this situation, but I acknowledge the fact that the Greater One lives on the inside of me.

"So, Father, I ask You right now through the power of the Holy Ghost who resides in me that You allow the wisdom and the understanding regarding this situation to well up and come to me." The Bible says wisdom shall be given to the person who prays this way.

The other day I talked to a preacher friend of mine who is involved in a terrible legal battle. He was heavy-hearted. I prayed with him over the phone, encouraged him in the Lord, and hung up.

Later, as I was getting ready for bed, an idea welled up in me — right out of my spirit — and I said to myself, "Wait a minute!"

I called my friend back and said, "Guess what? I just got a word of knowledge about your situation. This is what it is…" My friend said, "I'm going to call my lawyer right now." His lawyer said, "My God, that's it! We'll do it."

Where did that strategy come from? It was the wisdom of God that's in me by the Holy Ghost.

Lawyers go to law school and just learn law. Unless your lawyer is full of the Holy Ghost, he only knows how to do natural things. You have to contribute the supernatural part to the solution.

Walking in Christ

Notice that Paul told us to let our hearts be comforted and knit together in love and to acknowledge the mystery of God, "in whom are hid all the treasures of wisdom and understanding" (Colossians 2:2,3). Why? Let's read further. Verse 4 says, "And this I say lest any man should beguile you with enticing words."

God is going to keep His Word. I don't have to worry about it. I am comforted, praise God. The devil has been defeated, and I don't have to worry about him, because He's under my feet. I am going to walk in the love of God.

I am going to acknowledge that everything I need for my journey is already in God, who is in me, and the wisdom and the understanding I need will come up as I need them. And I am going to guard myself from enticing words that beguile.

Paul continues in verse 5 and 6, "For though I be absent in the flesh, yet am I with you in the spirit, joying and beholding your order, and the steadfastness of your faith in Christ. As ye have therefore received Christ Jesus the Lord, so walk ye in him."

If you put it in today's English, Paul was saying, "In the same manner you received Christ, walk in Christ."

Here's how I received Christ. With my heart I believed unto righteousness — but I was not saved until confession was made unto salvation with my mouth. (See Romans 10:10.)

As you have believed with your heart on the Lord Jesus Christ and confessed Him, receiving Him into your life, keep on believing and confessing what He says. That's how you walk in Christ.

You had to believe Jesus and confess Him as the *Savior* of your spirit before you were saved. Why, then, do you struggle to believe and confess Him as the *Healer* of your body while you're experiencing symptoms?

Religion's Beguiling Words

Why do you have a problem believing that every good and perfect gift comes from God, and He is a God who blesses? It's because you stop with salvation. Religion has vain words that beguile you.

Religion has indoctrinated you to believe that although God cannot lie about His promises regarding your eternal salvation, He doesn't mean His promises regarding your physical healing or your financial blessing! Religion has indoctrinated you to believe that God just picks and chooses who will receive His promises.

That's the most ridiculous thing I've ever heard! If God were like that, He would be the most schizophrenic being in the universe. But He's not!

Paul continues his teaching in Colossians 2:

As ye have therefore received Christ Jesus the Lord, so walk in him:

Rooted and built up in him, and established in the faith, as ye have been taught, abounding therein with thanksgiving.

Beware lest any man spoil you through philosophy and vain deceit, after the tradition of men, after the rudiments of the world, and not after Christ.

For in him dwelleth all the fulness of the Godhead bodily.

Colossians 2:6-9

How the Devil "Spoils" You

Notice the words "beware" and "spoil you." How do you *spoil* someone? It's when you take their possessions, treasures, or wealth. Notice how the devil spoils you. The Bible says we wrestle not against flesh and blood, so it's not really men spoiling you; it's what men *say* that spoils you.

Where do philosophy and vain deceit come from? The Bible says there is a wisdom that is divine, and there is a wisdom that is satanic or hellish. So there are only two sources of wisdom, and one is far inferior to the other.

Sometimes philosophy sounds pretty good. However, if you listen to the wrong philosophical sermons, words of vain deceit, traditions of men, and rudiments of the world, you could lose whatever you've got in God — because *words have power!* Those kinds of words could "spoil" you.

You have been rooted and built up, Paul says, and you have something that can be spoiled. You are commanded by God to guard it, lest men spoil you through vain deceit.

Coming Out of Your Country

When Jesus said, "Give, and it *shall* — not might, not could, but shall — be given unto you," the first thing you must do is stop thinking *how,* or you'll never come out of your country.

Your culture hasn't taught you, "Give, and it shall be given unto you." Your culture has taught you, "Keep, and you'll have what you've got." Your culture never taught you that spiritual laws work.

The enemy doesn't want the Church to believe certain laws. It's all right to believe God is *able* to bless you, and it's all right to believe God *can* bless you, but if you believe it's a *law,* you'll be persecuted and resisted. People won't like it, because the devil doesn't want people to understand it is a law.

If Jesus said, "Give, and it shall be given unto you," either He's a liar and isn't any better than the rest of humanity, or He was telling the truth. But I'll tell you, I wasn't saved by a liar! It wasn't a liar who broke the bondage of drug addiction off my life. Jesus can't lie. He's the way, the truth, and the life. I've settled it in my mind.

It's a Law

I don't ask, "If I give, how is it going to be given to me?" That's not my job. It's a law.

Someone may ask, "Do you really think it will be given to you?" Are you calling Jesus a liar?

"Well, God might not want you to have something, because He can't trust you with it." That's true, but giving *qualifies* a person to receive, because you can't give unless you trust God — and you can't trust God unless you love Him. What will you do with money when it comes? If you love God, you'll give part or all of it away anyway!

God will take care of you. He cannot lie. Therefore, the first thing you must do is give — and it will be given to you. And you shouldn't care how it comes. Just remember, it's a law.

I recently cleaned out my closet and gave away rings, watches, and clothing. Four weeks later, I got a bookstore for our church. People who don't understand giving will look at our new building and say, "Look what Christian Harfouche did with the people's money!" The people's money didn't buy the bookstore. It was Luke 6:38 that brought it in.

Give, and it shall be given unto you.

"Do you think it will happen?" Certainly it will happen.

"How do you *know* it's going to happen?" Did the sun come up today."

"Yes." Were you expecting it? Will the sun set tonight? Will you expect that? Are you sure it's going to happen? Do the tides go out and come in? Does your hair grow? Those things are all regulated by laws.

"Give, and it shall be given unto you" is also a law that works for everyone.

How God Will Finance the Kingdom

Some say, "We give, but we really don't expect anything in this life." You've got a problem. Jesus said, *"Men shall give into your bosom."* Notice He didn't say God or angels would give to you; He said *men* would give to you,

"Good measure, pressed down, and shaken together, and running over, shall men give into your bosom." It's a law!

For everything I'm giving, many things are coming to me — basketfuls, truckloads full. People who do not plan to give anything to me suddenly get an urge to give! That's how God will finance the kingdom. And that's the subject of this book.

We are not discussing accumulating material things for the sake of having things. Don't forget, when the Rapture happens, we won't be taking any of our earthly possessions with us anyway!

The same people who criticize the prosperity message have money stashed away for a rainy day. They don't realize it's already raining! God is pouring out the latter rain on us.

Many of these people accuse the prosperity message of being a message of materialism. But when was the last time you saw a person who was both giving *and* materialistic?

I never ran into a materialistic person who said, "We need $1000 for the ministry. Do you want to give?" That kind of person is not going to give, because money is his or her god. So how can you be materialistic and be a giving person at the same time?

The Promise of Harvest

However, you can be foolish. You can give and expect nothing — and you'll run out of money. Then you'll have to lean on someone who understands the principle of sowing and reaping so they can help you, because you don't understand the latter part of Luke 6:38.

Some will say, "God just wants you to give and not expect anything in return." Then why did Jesus say, "Give, and it shall be given unto you"? That is His promise!

Notice Jesus spent more time describing the harvest than He did the seed. He just said, "Give." That was it.

It's a "done deal." Then He described the harvest: "...it shall be given unto you...."

If Jesus spent a lot of time describing the harvest, you must keep the harvest in mind. You must come out of your kindred.

I used to live where you keep, bury, or lose your seed, but now I'm out of that country. I'm over here where you sow and receive with the same measure you mete out. Isn't that awesome?

Treasures Out of the Heart

I've learned there are two things we must do: First, we've got to sow our seed and keep in mind that a harvest is coming. Second, we've got to keep our confession in our mouth, because it says in Luke 6:45:

> **A good man out of the good treasure of his heart bringeth forth that which is good; and an evil man out of the evil treasure of his heart bringeth forth that which is evil: for of the abundance of the heart his mouth speaketh.**

This says that what is in you will come out in the form of *words*, because out of the abundance of the heart the mouth speaks. What is in your heart in abundance? What you believe!

Confession is nothing more than saying what you believe.

Some people think confession is an attempt to manipulate God, but that's ridiculous. You've first got to believe God before you say what He says. And the only reason for your not saying what He says is, you don't believe Him!

A good man out of the good treasure brings forth good things. What is the treasure? What you believe.

Expectant Givers

What is the believer commanded to believe? "Thy word have I hid in my heart..." (Psalm 119:11). If you hide God's Word in your heart, what comes out when you open your mouth? The Word. And what does His Word say? It says, "Give."

If someone asks, "Dr. Harfouche, how is your ministry doing in Pensacola," what's wrong if I reply, "We're doing very well, praise God. We are givers — we give continually — and God gives back to us good measure, pressed down, shaken together, and running over.

"Truckloads of equipment are coming. Resources are coming. Finances are coming. Money is coming from everywhere to help us fulfill our vision!"

Although people see this happen, they don't fully understand it, because they have never encountered anyone who put God's Word in his heart. Because of that, it has affected the way they see things. They no longer cry about the seed they've sown and lost. Now they see the harvest that is coming.

Jesus described it clearly. *Men* are bringing your harvest. It's pressed down. It's shaken together. It's a good measure. And it's running over!

If the Word of God is in you in abundance, it will come out of your mouth. The only good treasure you can have is the treasure of the Word of God, which brings forth good things. What are the good things you bring forth? Out of the abundance of the heart, the mouth speaks. The things you're bringing forth are speaking. The good man speaks what is in his heart in abundance.

After You Tithe

On the other hand, you may find a wonderful Christian brother, and when you ask, "How are you doing," he might say, "Oh, my brother, not so good. Things are terrible. Unless the Lord does something, I'm sunk!"

When I meet someone like this, I always ask, "Brother, are you sowing?" "Oh, yes, we give continually." "Are you tithing?" "Oh, yes, we're tithing."

What people like this need to do is skip the word "give" in Luke 6:38, because they've got that principle down. They need to go on and meditate on the latter phrase "and it shall be given unto you."

They need to settle it, because if Jesus said it, that's the way it is. Jesus talked about men giving to us. That means that before I die — not in the sweet by-and-by, but while I'm on Earth — while men still have an opportunity to sow seed into my life and ministry, they're going to bring it in by the truckloads! They're going to shovel it in! They're going to pile it up!

Keep Your Miracle in Motion!

Meditate on the Word of God until it's a treasure in your heart. Then, when someone comes knocking on the door of your life, and your mouth opens to answer, it doesn't answer with the rudiments of this world, philosophy, or the traditions of men and vain deceit. It answers by simply stating its *expectation*.

Do you know what that does? *It keeps your miracle in motion.*

A messenger can be coming with your miracle but be turned back when the devil asks you a question and you make a negative confession.

Are you facing a financial situation you need God to take care of? Many of us get to a place in life where not only all our *needs* are met, but we can also *abound* to every good work. It's going to happen. It's already happening to some. The door is wide open for everyone who is ready to get in on it.

Jesus said men will give to you. One translation says, "will He cause men." Notice He didn't say He would *force* men to give to you; He said He would *cause* them to give to you.

Now you know what God is doing: *He is giving you exactly what you expect.*

A Matter of Obedience

Sometimes we think, "If God wants to do it, then why doesn't He?" We think He's going to force someone to give it to us, but He has never forced anyone to do so. How does He cause men to give?

Obedience is an issue. We've got to *agree* to give. God may have to talk to 10 people who said no before He finds one who is willing to obey!

In your case, God may say, "I can't use his employer, because he is a hard-headed cheapskate, so I'm going to remove My child and put him into another situation where I can use him."

In my case, God passes up 10 men until He gets to Brother Jones. Brother Jones is obedient. He says, "Yes, I will do it. I'll help Dr. Harfouche." Now he's on the way to my house to give to me good measure, pressed down, shaken together, and running over.

However, while he's on the way, Sister Bucketmouth and Brother Unbelief call me on the telephone and talk about all kinds of doubt and unbelief. After I hang up, I feel a heaviness, because I didn't speak the Word of God. I say to God, "Are You ever going to do this? I just don't know if this thing is working."

Before I know it, with my own mouth I have proclaimed my lack of expectation for the thing I claim I believe. And God says, "According to your faith be it unto you!"

While Brother Jones is coming, he gets a check in his spirit, because there's no connection there anymore. My faith is not pulling on him anymore; neither is God saying, "Go do for him what's he's expecting."

However, God graciously bails you out of many of these situations, because He wants to show you He's a good God. Would you like God to come through every time you need Him? He will.

Ready To Be Blessed

God knows when you're ready to be blessed. For example, the Spirit of the Lord moved on Kenneth Copeland to give his airplane to a friend of his, but every time he started to, God would say, "No, don't do it yet."

At the same time, God was dealing with Brother Copeland's friend to get things right with another preacher friend. God told him, "Get your weeds off your seed."

Although he was sowing good seed, there was a problem between him and the other preacher that was short-circuiting the gift. He had a plane potentially on the way, but God was not going to give it to him unless he got things right in his heart.

Finally he talked to this other preacher. They got things squared away, prayed together, and released one another. That was the week the preacher got his airplane. The gift was on the way, but the Spirit of God stopped it for a month.

You must learn that walking with God means walking with Him in every area of your life, and you can't be blessed in one area unless you are committed in every area. When you are involved in the kingdom of God and His business, your heart must be right. And if you are covetous, you will end up losing everything.

Prayer

The treasures of wisdom and knowledge regarding life and godliness are in me. They are in Christ, and Christ is in me. And through prayer and the Word, this wisdom and this understanding will flow into my life and will help me live in the provision of God.

Revival and the glory of God must be funded by the silver and the gold. The finances I need will come in to pay my bills, get me out of debt, and help me support the ministries that are serving Jesus.

I will not fear. God has called me out of my kindred into another land. I will not speak against God's Word. My heart and my mouth will be in agreement, and I will see the fulfillment of His promises, in Jesus' Name.

Chapter 7
The Blood Erased the Curse!

The poor are not poor because God is "blessing" them with poverty. The poor are poor because poverty exists on Earth, and because the curse of poverty attaches itself to everyone who allows it — saint and sinner alike.

"Do you mean I'm poor because I'm no good?" I didn't say that. Some really good people are poor, and some really evil people are rich. The latter sold their souls for riches, but we are not studying riches; we are studying the silver, the gold, and the glory. We are studying about prosperity from God. We are studying about benefitting from what Jesus did when He came to Earth to sacrifice Himself for us two thousand years ago.

The Book of Hebrews tells us that when Jesus went into the heavenly Holy of Holies after His crucifixion, He didn't appear before God with the blood of sacrificial bulls or goats; He appeared before God with His own blood.

If Jesus spilled His blood for me to have something, I want it, even if I don't need it. I'd rather give it away than allow it to remain in the hands of the devil! If Jesus paid for it, I claim it, because His blood was spilled for a reason. He came to Earth to put away sin by the sacrifice of Himself.

The Source of Poverty

Where does poverty come from? It comes from the devil.

Did poverty come before man's sin or after man's sin? It came after man's sin.

Was poverty a promise or a consequence of sin? It was a consequence of sin. This means that poverty came as a result of the fall of man.

Why did God create man in His image and after His likeness? Why did God plant a garden that was full of every good fruit and every good tree and put man in it? Why didn't God put man in a poverty-stricken, dry desert to teach him something?

And why was man *wealthy* when God created him? After all, when you own the Garden of Eden, you're doing well!

The Consequences of Sin

However, when man sinned — when man fell from his place of union with God — several things happened to him that were the consequences of sin. God exiled him from the garden. He put him in a desolate place where he had to toil and fight for whatever he could get. The ground and the animal kingdom were cursed.

That's why the blood of a perfect sacrifice had to be shed. How many times was the blood shed? The Bible says that Jesus died *once* to put away sin by the sacrifice of Himself.

I happen to believe that God removed my sins as far as the East is from the West, because that is what the Word of God says. I believe He took everything I ever did wrong and threw it into "the sea of forgetfulness." There is no record of it. I have been justified by faith, and it's just as if I'd never sinned! If I don't have a record, why should I pay the penalty of poverty?

Not Qualified for Poverty

If the penalty of sin is poverty, our sin has been washed away by the blood of the Lamb, and we are now guiltless in the sight of God — *we no longer qualify for poverty!* Poverty is a consequence of unrighteousness or a lack of right-standing with God.

Religion has sold us a bill of lies. Religion has conditioned us to strip the blood of its power! Religion has denied the power of the blood. It has accused those of us who believe in it of being materialistic and money-hungry, when in reality it is God who takes the poor from the dust and the beggar from the dunghill to set them among princes and cause them to inherit the throne of glory. (See First Samuel 2:8.)

The same One who gives you the inheritance of the throne gives you the position to be seated with princes. Why? Because *it was the same sacrifice that paid for both!*

Some people think, "Maybe I'm not called to have my bills paid. Maybe the Lord doesn't want me to have anything." You must understand that your confidence comes from the fact that Jesus paid for it by His blood, and it had nothing to do with your personal performance. And you must understand, *poverty is a spirit!*

Expecting God's Will

If Jesus told me to pray, "Thy kingdom come. Thy will be done in earth, *as it is in heaven*," I must use heaven as a standard for the will of God.

"But, brother, you don't understand. I know someone in Arkansas..." Arkansas is not the standard. "I know someone in Los Angeles..." Los Angeles is not the standard. The standard is heaven. Therefore, it must be God's will for us to expect His will to be done on Earth the way it's done up there.

What does that mean? We are on a quest to experience a transformation in our lives that conforms with what Jesus did for us.

In other words, our lives should become more godly, more spiritual, more consistent, stronger, and more fruitful. And the more God can do this with individuals, the more He can do it with groups.

No Poverty in Heaven

"Thy will be done in earth, *as it is in heaven.*" What's heaven like? Heaven doesn't have any poverty. There's no record of anyone being caught up to the poor side of town and seeing unemployed angels standing in line.

There is no poverty in heaven because there are no demons there! They have all been kicked out. The problem is, they are down here on Earth with us! However, we have been given authority over them.

We must understand that poverty is the work of Satan.

We don't hate, dislike, or look down on poor people. We wouldn't be Christians if we did. We don't claim to be more spiritual than poor people. We'd be walking in pride if we did. You can't get saved unless you hear about salvation, because faith comes by hearing. And you can't prosper unless you hear about prosperity. The Bible says, "My people are destroyed [or perish] for lack of knowledge" (Hosea 4:6).

Cleansed From All Unrighteousness

Once we become born again and walk in the light as God is in the light, we have fellowship one with another, and the blood of Jesus Christ his Son cleanses us from all sin (1 John 1:7).

Notice the phrase "the blood." It was shed once. It won't be shed again. Jesus will not shed one more drop of blood. He has no more to shed. He shed it all. If the blood didn't do it the first time, you're in trouble. But the blood did it. It cleanses us from all unrighteousness.

If I have been cleansed from all unrighteousness, it means I must have been cleansed from Adam's original sin. I couldn't be saved unless I was forgiven — and I am forgiven. So if I'm forgiven, why should any Christian pay the consequences of what our backslidden granddaddy Adam did when he bowed the knee to the devil?

I was born again by the Spirit. And if I was born by the Spirit from above, I must seek the will of God on Earth the way it is up there in heaven.

Jesus is not coming back to die. He's not coming back to pay one cent more than what He already paid. If what He paid for us does not supply us with at least the same measure of success Old Testament patriarchs and saints had, something is wrong!

A Matter of Life or Death

The anointing blesses you. Therefore, the church you attend can be a matter of life or death to you. For example, if a person gets sick with a terminal disease, and he or she is attending the wrong church — a church where the Holy Ghost isn't allowed to move — you might as well make funeral arrangements for them. It's the truth.

People die in that atmosphere of doubt and unbelief unless they go to a meeting where God sovereignly, supernaturally moves and miracles happen. Once they are healed, they have to make up their mind, "How am I going to live my life from now on? Which church should I attend?"

Not only is it a matter of life or death which church you go to, it's also a matter of success or failure. Why? Because what is being ministered to you will either bring faith for *success* or faith for *failure*. Both faith and failure come by hearing.

It's also a matter of life or death which Bible school you attend. It's important whose teaching you sit under, because the words your teachers speak are either spirit and life or spirit and death! If they are words of truth, they are spirit and life, and they will feed your spirit for success.

Transference and Impartation

God called Abraham out of his kindred, and Abraham became the father of the faithful. In the Bible, Abraham is the picture of a successful, rich, healthy saint who enjoyed a long life. He was a patriarch.

Abraham laid hands on Isaac and *blessed* him through the transference of the laying on of hands. Jacob had the same God. Isaac laid hands on Jacob, and what happened? The same thing. Later, Joseph got the impartation. Despite the problems caused by his jealous brothers and Potiphar's wife, he ended up second only to pharaoh in Egypt.

Throughout the Bible you find a thread of transference and impartation from one ministry gift to another. All of it ends up resulting in financial success.

Why? Because *it is the will of God for His people to be the example of what He can do for you.* He doesn't want you to be a beggar. How could such a thing be when you are the child of the richest person in the universe? How could you say, "My Father owns the cattle on a thousand hills" and not have a few head of cattle yourself?

The Truth About Finances

The reason you are not enjoying financial success is because some ministers who are preaching to you are lying. They don't know the truth about prosperity themselves.

They think they've got to sell chicken dinners, sponsor bingo games, or hold car washes and other junk to raise money. They don't understand that the blood of Jesus Christ was spilled to erase sin and do away with the penalty of sin — which is poverty!

It's at this point that people miss it. They think that when you get money, you're blessed. But *money is not the blessing.* I know people who have money and also have ulcers because of worrying about how to keep their money.

Money is really nothing but a tool, yet the blessing makes you content. The blessing makes you secure. The blessing gives you favor. And when you have the favor of God, everything else is added. That addition is the result of the favor. *The blood of Jesus paid for the favor of God!*

Mary's Prophecy

Jesus did not come and die in vain; He died for a reason. We see this in Luke 1:46,47: "And Mary said, My soul doth magnify the Lord, and my spirit hath rejoiced in God my Saviour."

Mary said this because she had conceived Him. In Luke 1:48-55, she continues:

For he hath regarded the low estate of his handmaiden: for, behold, from henceforth all generations shall call me blessed.

For he that is mighty hath done to me great things; and holy is his name.

And his mercy is on them that fear him from generation to generation.

He hath shewed strength with his arm; he hath scattered the proud in the imagination of their hearts.

He hath put down the mighty from their seats, and exalted them of low degree.

He hath filled the hungry with good things; and the rich he hath sent empty away.

He hath holpen his servant Israel, in remembrance of his mercy;

As he spake to our fathers, to Abraham, and to his seed for ever.

Church, we'd better listen to these prophetic words in the New Testament, because they are relevant to us today.

I guarantee you that no virgin will ever again conceive and bear a son and call His name "Jesus." Since Mary has done that, and since God spoke through her prophetically, we'd better understand what she was saying.

What Mary Saw

Mary made those statements before the baby was even born, before the cross came, and before the price was paid. Yet she saw prophetically what the cross would accomplish, what the resurrection would bring, and how we would benefit.

Mary said that God has shown the strength of His arm. Do you know that Jesus demonstrated the most powerful display of God's power when He destroyed the power of darkness over all humanity? He spoiled principalities and powers. How did He do it? With the strength of His arm (Luke 1:51).

She said further, "He has scattered the proud." How? In the imagination of their hearts. Notice, it wasn't God who willed that the proud be scattered; the proud were scattered by the imagination of their own hearts.

As James wrote, "Let no man say when he is tempted, I am tempted of God: for God cannot be tempted with evil, neither tempteth he any man: But every man is tempted, when he is drawn away of his own lust, and enticed" (James 1:13,14). That means you can't share the blame with God for the things you do.

When you hear the truth but imagine something different, you must make a choice. If you shake your head religiously and say, "I just don't buy it," and you believe a lie, you get scattered with your own concept. Your vain imagination keeps you out of the flow of God's anointing.

The Spirit of God never flows contrary to God's Word.

The Spirit of God never flows contrary to God's will.

The Choice Is Yours

The proud have been scattered. How? With the imagination of their hearts. It wasn't God who gave them that imagination, because if He had, why would He tell them to cast down imaginations? And how could He hold them accountable for not casting down what He supposedly put in their hearts?

People are always faced with choices like this. One kind is a rational, natural, or even "religious" choice. The other is spiritual and divine, according to the will of God.

If Jesus paid for something, the Spirit of God wants to reveal that it belongs to you so you can fulfill what Jesus did on your behalf.

It is important for us in this day to understand these things, because if you vacate your responsibility to be blessed, someone else will be blessed and used — and God wants to use you.

Israel and the Heathen

In Luke 1:52, Mary spoke about the contrast between Israel and the heathen. God has pulled the heathen, the mighty, and the ungodly from their seats and exalted those of low degree, she prophesied.

Then you see in verse 54 that He helped Israel. So those of low degree were Israel, and those who were mighty and were brought down were the heathen, the Gentiles, or the world that rejects Christ.

Notice that a Jewish virgin was prophesying here. Even though she was prophesying about her nation, her prophecy is found in the New Testament.

I am a Gentile Christian. To me, Israel is not just an ancient nation. I see Israel as everyone who believes on Christ. To me, a Jew is not just one who is circumcised *physically;* a Jew is one who has been circumcised *spiritually* with the circumcision of the heart.

So I see this passage as God taking those of us who are of low estate — who are unsaved — and the moment we believe, He picks us up and promotes us.

Then the proud are scattered in the imagination of their hearts. Even when they are mighty, sitting in high places, they are brought down. How did that happen? It happened through Jesus' first coming — and the virgin prophesied it done.

Promotion and Financial Blessing

Today there are Christians sitting around watching Christian television, waiting for Gabriel to blow the trumpet. They are willing to leave the world to Antichrist, because they don't think we should own anything down here.

I'd rather give the silver and the gold away than leave it in the hands of the pornographer or the dope dealer. The blood was shed for it!

I'm going to believe for it, and it's going to come. Do you want it to come to you? Stick around, because just like Abraham gave it to Isaac, and Isaac gave it to Jacob, and Jacob gave it to Joseph, we're going to give it to you. That's how it works.

We read in verse 53, "He hath filled the hungry with good things; and the rich he hath sent empty away." The difference is: The hungry were hungry, so they got what they were hungry for!

And the next verses say, "He hath holpen [helped] his servant Israel, in remembrance of his mercy; as he spake to our fathers, to Abraham, and to his seed for ever" (verses 54,55). This is the foundation for deliverance from the curse, a deliverance that includes divine prosperity!

God spoke promotion and financial blessing to Abraham and his seed forever. Then Mary prophesied, "He showed His mighty arm; He scattered the proud; He picked up those of low degree; and He fed those who were hungry."

Promotion and financial blessing were thus attached to the first coming of the Lord Jesus Christ! The Early Church saw it prophetically as a "done deal." The battle was won on Calvary!

The nation of Israel looked forward to the coming of their Messiah. They believed that when He came, their problems would be solved forever. And He came — and our problems are solved. We just refuse to allow Him to perform as if they are.

We are too busy worrying about the problems and acting as if they are *not* solved. We have been spoiled through vain deceit. Religion has talked us out of what Jesus paid for two thousand years ago!

A Vow of Prosperity

Through the ages, certain groups of Christians have taken a vow of poverty. I think I'll take a vow of prosperity right now: "I am going to vow, Lord, that I am going to prosper in your Name. Praise God!"

People are always giving us things. People will give you things, too. Things will come into your life supernaturally. You've got to know this will happen for the kingdom of God.

Why? Because God wants you to benefit from what He paid for. All God's resources are in the Earth for us to use to preach the Gospel to every kingdom.

Feed your faith until you can believe for it!

Several years ago, I was believing God for a certain amount of money. I told my wife, Robin, "Before this thing is over, $100 million will be given to our ministry." That's where my faith is.

I don't care where it comes from. For all I care, some Arab sheik might call me and say, "You know, I was riding my camel the other day..." Many people want to do something good before they die. Someone might call me and say, "I saw one of your books. I am wiring you $100 million." I'll say, "Yes, thank you very much. I was just talking about that the other day when I made a vow of prosperity."

Do you know what we will do with all that money? We're going to put it into the work of the kingdom and snatch souls from the hands of the devil for the Lord Jesus!

God's Mercy

The Bible calls the promise God made to Abraham and his seed forever, His *mercy:* "He hath holpen his servant Israel, in remembrance of his mercy; as he spake to our fathers, to Abraham, and to his seed for ever."

When blind Bartimaeus saw Jesus and said, "Son of David, have mercy on me!" that was included in the promise God gave to Abraham when He said, "In your seed, Abraham, shall all the nations of the earth be blessed."

Poor, blind Bartimaeus had enough religious sense to know that if this Jesus is the seed of Abraham, and he calls for mercy, mercy and blessing will go hand-in-hand. And mercy includes his deliverance from blindness as well as from poverty!

So Bartimaeus ripped his coat off, threw it down, walked over to Jesus, and said, "Lord, that I might receive my sight." And God delivered him from two aspects of the curse at one time! God called that His mercy. He is a merciful God. You just need to develop a little more faith in His consistency.

Redeemed From the Curse and Poverty

We read in Galatians 3:13,14, "Christ hath redeemed us from the curse of the law, being made a curse for us: for it is written, Cursed is every one that hangeth on a tree: That the blessing of Abraham might come on the Gentiles through Jesus Christ; that we might receive the promise of the Spirit through faith."

You cannot read the word "redeemed" without understanding that redemption comes by the blood of Jesus Christ. And if Christ has already redeemed us, it's a "done deal." If it's not a "done deal," He would have to pay for it in the future; but because He has redeemed us, He paid for it in the past — once and for all!

What did Christ redeem us *from?* The Bible says He redeemed us from the curse of the Law. What did He redeem us *to?* Many of us get redeemed from the curse, but we don't go on to the next verse, which says, "That *the blessing of Abraham* might come on the Gentiles through Jesus Christ."

Many don't understand that the blood paid for deliverance from the poverty that is a by-product of the curse.

After Christ delivered us, here comes the blessing of Abraham. The Bible calls this His mercy. He remembered His mercy, which is the blessing He promised Abraham and his seed forever. We are the seed and are therefore entitled to His mercy!

Mercy helps the poor, and when God blesses you, you help the poor. After you've helped them materially, you should teach them that the anointing will help them and can blast poverty out of their lives forever!

Poverty doesn't leave you when you get money. Some very wealthy people are poverty-stricken. They're poor in their minds and poor in their conduct, because they serve their money.

So poverty doesn't leave you when money comes; *poverty leaves you before you ever own a thing.* When you realize you've been delivered from the curse of the Law, you're no longer poor. You're rich before you ever get a cent. You're rich because you've got the blessing. You're a child of God.

How the Anointing Flows

I've learned something in the ministry. In our early days, Robin and I traveled all over the world when we didn't have a local church behind us and when we did have a local church behind us — but they didn't exactly believe the way we believe.

Although they prayed for us when we were on the road, we ran into some extremely difficult situations. We fought battles we didn't need to fight; we went through financial situations we didn't need to go through; and we used all of our faith to get a little bit of the Word of God to work for us.

We believed then what we believe now. This is what we have believed ever since Robin and I have been together. And before we met and got married, this is what I believed.

The way the anointing flows is found in Psalm 133:1-3.

Behold, how good and how pleasant it is for brethren to dwell together in unity!

143

It is like the precious ointment [or anointing] upon the head, that ran down upon the beard, even Aaron's beard: that went down to the skirts of his garments:

As the dew of Hermon, and as the dew that descended upon the mountains of Zion: for there the Lord commanded the blessing, even life for evermore.

One translation reads, "It is from here that men will be blessed forever." And notice it is upon the mountains of Zion. This refers to the Church. Notice where the anointing is poured: It is like the precious ointment upon the head. And the key is: "Behold, how pleasant it is for brethren to dwell together in unity."

The only unity you can have in your body is with your head. Your body is in unity with your head. Some people talk with their hands. Their hands are in unity with their thoughts.

The point is: *God uses unity as an example of how the anointing flows.* Where is the anointing poured? It's poured on the pastor's head. It's poured on the vision of the ministry.

Every one of us is also a "head" of something. You may be the head of a business, or you may be the head of a home. If the husband won't assume his responsibilities and is not serving God, the anointing will be poured on the wife.

Although each of us has his or her own anointing, there is an area called "government" or spiritual alignment that we can't violate. When we get out of our calling, we get out of sync with God.

For example, if a woman is not submitted to her husband, she gets out of sync. If a husband is domineering, he gets out of sync. The anointing always flows from the top down. The anointing gets on our children, too.

Don't Fix the Pastor

Most people try to fix what's "up there" rather than fix what's "down there." Most people want to fix the pastor. You can't fix the pastor.

Either God fixes the pastor, or the pastor's friends fix the pastor. And if the pastor doesn't have the right friends and the right relationship with God, you've got no business trying to fix him! You need to go to a church that has the right kind of pastor, and one who has the anointing flowing on him or her.

When the anointing flows down, it gives you the ability to take care of whatever is in your area of influence.

We read, "How good and how pleasant it is for brethren to dwell together in unity!" This could be anywhere, but it's actually a kind of place or atmosphere. Where unity is — where agreement is — God gets things done. Where there is no agreement, God gets less done.

That's what happened to us when the churches praying for us were not in complete agreement with us. We would be out on the road, and although people were praying for us, we were running into many controversial situations, because our prayer covering didn't have the kind of revelation or anointing that could propel us into what we were doing in God. Thus, we had to fight two battles, and we felt it in the Spirit.

The Importance of Agreement

Now we have our own church in Pensacola, Florida, backing us with prayer, and it never fails us. Our members get together on Wednesday evenings and pray, and God shakes the place. When Robin and I are out of town holding crusades, on Wednesday evenings, at about the time our people finish praying, the crusade meetings break wide open; and on Thursday mornings, without fail, we have a great move of God.

Imagine what would happen if we were all in agreement with the vision of our pastors! Talk about the place where God commanded the blessing! He said, "It is from here that men will be blessed forever."

The spiritual atmosphere of unity causes the favor and the blessing of God to abound. That anointing falling down flows from one member to another and to another, and things happen as a result. This is how the anointing and the glory work together.

You can't have brethren dwelling together in unity unless they think and say the same thing. The first thing the devil does to destroy people's lives is to get them in disagreement with the vision of God that is being preached to them.

There is a famine in the land. Sometimes I flip through the Christian television stations — and I don't mean to criticize — but it's rare to tap into any teaching of substance. And I've traveled extensively and been in all kinds of churches.

Guarding the Vision

It's difficult to get under the right vision, but once you find it, the first step is to guard it. Why? Because when you hear it, and it brings faith to you, the devil comes to steal what is said to you.

He will ask questions you don't know the answers to, to get you to talk about things you've got no business talking to him about. He will get you to concentrate on minor issues. He will get you to question areas you've got no authority in and ignore areas in which you have authority.

The anointing guards the unity. When you run into something contrary to the Word of God, say, "That's not where I'm headed. I'm part of a body, a church, and we don't do that. We don't fail." The anointing will work. Just try it!

"Choice Things" Will Come

Let's look at Haggai 2:6-8 once again:

For thus saith the Lord of hosts; Yet once, it is a little while, and I will shake the heavens, and the earth, and the sea, and the dry land;

And I will shake all nations, and the desire of all nations shall come: and I will fill this house with glory, saith the Lord of hosts.

146

The silver is mine, and the gold is mine, saith the Lord of hosts.

God said He's going to shake the heavens, Earth, and the sea. Then He's going to shake all nations, and the desire of all nations shall come.

That word "desire" is translated as "choice things" in the *Septuagint:* "And I will convulse all nations, and the choice things of all nations will come, and I will fill this house with glory, says the Lord Almighty."

The choice things of all nations will come. Why will they come? Because God is going to shake the nations that possess those choice things!

Sometimes when God talks about nations in His Word, He is referring to families, like when He told Abraham, "...In thee shall all *families* of the earth be blessed" (Genesis 12:3; 28:14). But other versions read, "In thee shall all the *nations* of the earth be blessed." So God refers to families and nations almost interchangeably, and you must determine the correct meaning from the text.

God was saying once more, "I'm going to shake everything. And when I shake everything, the goodly things will come, and I am going to fill My house with glory." "The goodly things" refer to possessions.

The *King James Version* calls them "the desire of all nations." The *New English Bible* calls them "the treasures of all the nations." That means the things the nations have desired and acquired.

A Great Transference of Wealth

Then God said, "The silver is mine, and the gold is mine, and I will fill this house with glory. The glory of this latter house will be greater than the first. The treasures of all nations will come in."

We often quote Matthew 24:14: "And this gospel of the kingdom shall be preached in all the world for a witness unto all nations; and then shall the end come." But how many billions of dollars do you think it's going to take to preach the Gospel to every village on planet Earth?

The *New English Bible* says, "In this place, I will grant prosperity. This is the very word of the Lord." Notice Haggai 2:9: "The glory of this latter house shall be greater than of the former, saith the Lord of hosts: and in this place will I give peace, saith the Lord of hosts."

We know from both the *Septuagint* and the *New English Bible* that God was not only talking about shaking; He was talking about a great transference of wealth that would be coming into His house.

If what scatters me is the imagination of my heart, I am supposed to stop imagining vain things and start believing the Word of God. If I want to qualify for this transference of wealth, I've got to believe for it. If I don't, I won't receive it. I'll reject it. If I don't, it will pass me by, and I will miss out!

Shaking Treasures Loose

We're going to find out how God shakes, when God shakes, and why God shakes. He said He's only going to shake all nations once. "Yet once" is what He said. As a result of one shaking, the treasures of the nations are going to come in to His house!

Hebrews 12:22 begins, "But ye are come unto mount Sion...." Isn't that what we just read in Psalm 133: "It is from here that men will be blessed forever." That's the place where unity and agreement cause the anointing to flow from the head down until prosperity is the order of the day. It is in the New Testament as well!

> But ye are come unto mount Zion, and unto the city of the living God, the heavenly Jerusalem, and to an innumerable company of angels,
>
> To the general assembly and church of the firstborn, which are written in heaven, and to God the Judge of all, and to the spirits of just men made perfect.

And to Jesus the mediator of the new covenant, and to the blood of sprinkling, that speaketh better things than that of Abel.

Hebrews 12:22-24

Notice that there is an innumerable company of angels. You can't see them, but there are more angels on Earth than you can ever imagine, and they've got a job to do. When we operate in the Spirit realm, we operate in the realm of innumerable angels.

Why would we need innumerable angels if all they do is twiddle their thumbs? There's a reason why there are innumerable angels, and there's a reason why they're down here. God has sent His angels to help us in these last days. They only twiddle their thumbs when we do not command them to do what they are supposed to do.

The Blood of Sprinkling

Notice in verse 24 that it is "the blood of sprinkling" that speaks. The Bible says, "...having our hearts sprinkled from an evil conscience, and our bodies washed with pure water" (Hebrews 10:22). The Bible also says, "How much more shall the blood of Christ, who through the eternal Spirit offered himself without spot to God, purge your conscience from dead works to serve the living God" (Hebrews 9:14).

Those two scriptures are about conscience. We are supposed to be sprinkled from an evil conscience. We must be sprinkled to have a good or clear conscience. How do we get sprinkled to a clear conscience? We must hear what the blood is saying, because it's the blood of sprinkling that speaks.

Do you know what the blood says to me? It says, "Forgiveness." It says, "Your debt is cancelled; no revenge is required." It's not like the blood of Abel that says, "Get him, Lord — he killed me!" Instead, it's the blood of Jesus that says, "Forgive them, Father. They know not what they do." It speaks better things.

That's very important, because if my debt is cancelled, the penalty is cancelled. I'm not on parole. I'm not even on probation. The case has been dismissed. We won, and we continue to win!

What the Blood Speaks

If the blood of sprinkling speaks, we'd better listen to what it says. Hebrews 12:25,26 says, "See that ye refuse not him that speaketh. For if they escaped not who refused him that spake on earth, much more shall not we escape, if we turn away from him that speaketh from heaven: Whose voice then shook the earth...."

Do you mean Christ is speaking by His blood? Do you mean that all of a sudden men will get a revelation and preachers will finally preach what the blood paid for? Do you mean that all of a sudden preachers will stop preaching from Earth and start preaching from heaven?

The writer of Hebrews is not talking about an audible voice shouting from above to shake things up. He is talking about the Spirit of God inspiring revelation, causing the Word to live; and, all of a sudden, preachers beginning to speak what the blood has been saying.

We are not going to refuse Him that speaks from above. The blood is speaking good things: "Forgive." "Case dismissed." "The curse has been reversed." "You've been redeemed."

"Whose voice then shook the earth: but now *he hath promised*, saying, *Yet once more* I shake not the earth only, but also heaven" (Hebrews 12:26). Where else did God promise "yet once more"? We just read it in Haggai, but in the New Testament passage, He tied the shaking to the blood. He promised! We just need to prepare ourselves to receive the blessings.

All Things Will Be Shaken

And He said, "And this word, Yet once more, signifieth the removing of those things that are shaken, as of things

150

that are made, that those things which cannot be shaken may remain. Wherefore we receiving a kingdom which cannot be moved..." (Hebrews 12:27,28).

The author of Hebrews is saying the only thing that will not shake when the prophetic Word is preached from above — the only thing that will not shake when the Spirit of God fills the tongues and hearts of men with power — is the kingdom that cannot be shaken. That means every other kingdom will be shaken.

When does God shake? In New Testament days.

Why does God shake? So that the things that can be removed will be removed.

What things does God shake? God said, "I will shake all nations, and the desire [or the treasures] of all nations shall come." Why? Because they can be shaken.

Do you know why God is shaking them? He's shaking the wealth from the hands of the wicked and bringing it into the kingdom of God.

Everything that can be removed will be removed. Removed from where? Removed from the hands of the wicked and brought into the hands of the just so that we can use it to preach the Gospel of the kingdom.

One more time, let's review Haggai 2:6-8:

For thus saith the Lord of hosts; Yet once, it is a little while, and I will shake the heavens, and the earth, and the sea, and the dry land;

And I will shake all nations, and the desire of all nations shall come: and I will fill this house with glory, saith the Lord of hosts.

The silver is mine, and the gold is mine, saith the Lord of hosts.

In the Latter Days

What house is mentioned in this passage? Some say, "It was Solomon's Temple," or "It was some other temple." There is a problem with that, because God ties it in to the blood of Jesus. That takes it into the New Testament, so it can't be that. It couldn't be fulfilled under the Old Covenant dispensation.

Instead, we must look forward to a time when some shaking will take place. And if God ties it to the blood of Jesus, it couldn't be post-millennial, post-tribulation, or post-Rapture. It must be in the latter of the last days.

So God said, "And this word, Yet once more, signifieth the removing of those things that are shaken..." (Hebrews 12:27). Can you see it? This world is losing its grip. This signifies the removing of those things that can be shaken so the things which cannot be shaken may remain. What are the things which cannot be shaken? The things of the kingdom of God!

We have misunderstood what God is saying. We have thought, "God is going to shake things out of my life." Yes, He shakes things out of your life, but if your life is built on the Word of God, and you're only allowing in your life what the kingdom of God has brought into your life, what could be shaken out of your life?

Why would God shake my money when I already give it to Him? If God owns me, He's got to shake me out of His hand — and He's not going to do that.

So what are the things that can be shaken? God said, "I will shake all nations, and the desire of all nations shall come."

The Wealth of the Wicked Is Ours

Exciting discoveries and technological breakthroughs are currently taking place, and the devil thinks he's going to use them. But all of these discoveries and technological breakthroughs are waiting to be shaken out of the world's hands right into the kingdom of God.

I see television cameras, satellites, satellite dishes, trucks, machines, airplanes, buildings, resources, and finances

— and they're all coming into the kingdom! Coming, coming, coming, coming! You're going to see them come.

"See that ye refuse not him that speaketh...Whose voice then shook the earth: but now he hath promised, saying, Yet once more I shake not the earth only, but also heaven" (Hebrews 12:25,26). There's a whole lot of shaking going on. Glory to God! Shake it loose, Lord!

However, I don't want the wealth of the wicked unless it can be shaken loose. I want the world to keep every penny God can't shake loose; but I want everything that *can* be shaken loose to come into the kingdom of God. And it's going to come.

"The silver is mine, and the gold is mine," God said, "and I will fill this house with glory."

Build on the Rock

Whatever I build on the Word of God can't be shaken. If the house on the rock can't be shaken, the furniture in the house can't be shaken, either. When the floods come and the winds blow, and they beat on that house, it shall neither fall nor be flooded. It can't be shaken.

It can't fall, because it was never built on the sand of human ability. It was built on the kingdom of God and the Word of God. You can bank on the kingdom of God. It can't be shaken.

"...Let us have grace, whereby we may serve God acceptably with reverence and godly fear..." (Hebrews 12:28). Notice we don't just serve God; we should have the grace to serve Him *acceptably*.

What is grace? Unmerited ability. We say, "God, give me grace to serve You prosperously." God says, "Have grace."

When does God shake things? Under the New Covenant. Why does God shake things? So He can get them loose. How does God shake things? By His Word. But God says, "See that you refuse Him not."

153

That means that not all Christians are going to allow the transaction into their lives. While the treasures of nations are coming, some will, in their own thought life, wonder, "It just sounds too good to be true. How in the world will it ever happen to someone like me?" Small-mindedness refuses to accept God's promises of prosperity, and when it does, it locks out the benefits of the universal transaction that God will accomplish.

Our Needs Will Be Met

Every one of us will receive what God has for us according to our place in the kingdom. Not everyone will be a millionaire, but not everyone needs to be a millionaire. But everyone needs his or her needs met.

There will be those who will get into a great arena of responsibility in the kingdom of God. They will inherit things by virtue of divine transactions, because they had faith to believe. It will happen quickly. It will come upon you like a whirlwind.

The recipients will have to be sober and intelligent. They will have to control their minds and emotions, because when that kind of wealth flows through you, all kinds of darts will be launched from the enemy. You'll step into an arena of warfare you've never known before, and you'd better be ready to govern what God has put into your hands.

They're coming — the resources are coming!

God was speaking prophetically and by faith in Haggai. The silver is His, and the gold is His, even though legally at that time, they were universally in the hands of the enemy.

In Israel, the blood of animals was used for sacrifices, looking forward to the blood of Jesus, the perfect sacrifice. The Jews had a covenant with God; and God was able through that covenant, which was based on inferior promises, to salvage resources and blessings to fund that nation.

When the devil tempted Jesus in the wilderness, he said to Him, "Do you see these kingdoms and the glory of them? I'll give them to You if You bow down and worship me, because they are mine. They were delivered to me, and to whomsoever I will, I give them" (Luke 4:5-7 paraphrased). They were still in the hands of the enemy.

But Colossians tells us Jesus spoiled principalities (Colossians 2:15). Through His death, burial, and resurrection, Jesus took back legally everything the devil had stolen from mankind.

Therefore, in Haggai, God was speaking by faith when He said, "The silver is mine, and the gold is mine." In Hebrews 12, He says, "The blood is doing the talking."

That means that *every ounce of silver and gold on planet Earth has been paid for by the blood of Jesus!* It's the truth!

That's exciting, because it tells me the blood that was spilled paid for it, giving me the legal right to come in agreement with the blood. I'm not going to refuse Him that speaks.

When we get to heaven, who knows what the economy will be like, or what we will need to operate. Until then, we've got a job to fulfill on Earth for the kingdom, and we need money to accomplish it.

If God can say way back in Haggai that the silver and the gold are His, by faith I can get excited about getting it before I have it!

Chapter 8

Paid in Full!

The transference of wealth that is currently taking place will continue, should the Lord tarry, well into the first years of the new millennium.

However, we don't believe Jesus is going to tarry that long. We think He's coming very soon. And we believe there's a mighty revival taking place now that will sweep the whole world before Gabriel blows the trumpet!

We believe this great transference of finances is not coming just to take care of our personal needs. That's the easy part. It is coming to finance the kingdom of God. You can see from this perspective that we're not materialistic. If we were, we wouldn't be planning to leave the planet when Jesus returns.

You must understand that Christianity does not mean being under the control of God; instead, Christianity means being in *agreement* with Him. Simply put, Christianity does not control your life; instead, you realize that you are a steward over your life. That's important to remember if you're ever to step into the blessings and benefits of the New Testament.

Manifestations of the Kingdom

Do you have some needs in your life? Jesus said, "Seek ye first the kingdom of God, and his righteousness; and *all* these things shall be added unto you" (Matthew 6:33).

You don't seek the kingdom by saying, "Where is it? I'd like to find it. One day I'm going to get there." The kingdom of God does not come with observation. The Word of God teaches that the lordship of the Spirit is the manifestation of the kingdom.

Jesus taught us to pray, "Thy kingdom come, thy will be done in earth, as it is in heaven" (Matthew 6:10). There will come a day when Jesus comes to physically establish His kingdom on Earth. Until then, we are called by God to experience manifestations of God's will — little glimpses, little foresights, little experiences of what God intends to do in the near future.

The point is: If you put God and His Word first, everything you need will be supplied. So if you care more about building God's kingdom than you care about your own ambitions, you will be taken care of.

For example, I needed a computer for myself. I wanted one, but I didn't stay up nights asking God for one. I could have gone out and bought a computer, but I just thought, "It would be nice to have one." I didn't tell anyone about my wish.

One night, a friend of mine asked, "Do you have a computer?" I said, "Well, no, but I'm thinking of getting one." He said, "I've got a computer for you." And it's a good one. That's how that principle of Scripture works. That computer was "added" to me. I didn't go out seeking it; I sought the kingdom.

Although I could have bought a computer, I sought and pursued the kingdom instead. As a result, something was added to me. That's just one example of the many things that have come into my life like that.

A New Relationship

Continuing our study of Hebrews 12, let's read verses 22-25 again:

But ye are come unto mount Zion, and unto the city of the living God, the heavenly Jerusalem, and to an innumerable company of angels,

To the general assembly and church of the firstborn, which are written in heaven, and to God the Judge of all, and to the spirits of just men made perfect,

And to Jesus the mediator of the new covenant, and to the blood of sprinkling, that speaketh better things than that of Abel.

See that ye refuse not him that speaketh. For if they escaped not who refused him that spake on earth, much more shall not we escape, if we turn away from him that speaketh from heaven.

As you read this, make this confession: "This is the Word of God, not an opinion or a tradition, and it is not subject to debate. It's alive. God said it, I believe it, and that settles it. It is what it says it is. It will do what it says it will do. I am what it says I am. I have what it says I have. And if I believe it, I can do what it says I can do."

This passage says that when we are born again, we enter into a relationship with God. We come to the Church. We become a member of the house of God. The Church is a place where there are so many angels, they can't be counted. It's a place called Mount Zion (or Zion), the city of the living God. It's the General Assembly of the Firstborn.

Jesus, the One Mediator

Then, verse 24 says, we came to Jesus, "the mediator of the new covenant." That word "mediator" appears several times in the New Testament, and each reference is derived from the same Greek word. It's a key word, because until you understand what a "mediator" is, you can't benefit from what Jesus is mediating.

For example, the Bible says there is *one* mediator between God and man, the man Christ Jesus (1 Timothy 2:5). New Agers don't know that. They think there are many mediators between God and man. They try to get to God through whomever they think is the "door" to Him, but this line of thinking doesn't work.

Buddhists think Buddha is the door, and Muslims think Mohammed is the door. But you can't come to God unless you know that Jesus is the only way to Him. Not only is Jesus the only way to God; He is the only way to *you*. In other words, God can't bring anything into your life unless He brings it through Jesus Christ.

The Bible says that God is merciful, and He is a liberal giver. He causes His sun to rise on the just (the godly) and the unjust (the ungodly). His rain also falls on the just and the unjust.

God couldn't do that unless Jesus had given His life freely for everyone. Thus, even the blessings the ungodly receive are from God through His acknowledgment of what Christ did on Calvary.

You may wonder if this ties in with the silver, the gold, and the glory. It does. The reason why the majority of church members are poverty-stricken is because they don't know how to "cash in" on what Jesus was mediating for.

Getting in Agreement

Jesus is the mediator of what? The New Covenant. *The Twentieth Century* translation calls Him "the intermediary of a New Covenant." The *King James Version* calls Him "the mediator of the new covenant [agreement]."

An "agreement" cannot be an *agreement* unless it's between two parties. That means this book is not an "agreement" to you unless you are in agreement with it.

In times past, publishing houses have sent agreements to me. The conditions were typed out, and the agreements were signed by the owners of the publishing companies. These agreements included policies, percentages, and other financial information. Yet none of the agreements was a valid "agreement" until I signed it.

The Bible calls Jesus the intermediary of this new agreement between God and man, but most Christians want to live under the old agreement. They go back to the old agreement and wonder why the new agreement doesn't work for them. I want to live by the new agreement, because God has updated His files.

God hasn't changed, but God's relationship and dealings with man have changed. Why? Because God now has to deal with man through what Jesus accomplished on the cross; through what the blood of Jesus bought on Calvary; and through what the stripes of Jesus paid for.

God must deal with man through the cross — and He wants to. He wants to so much, He gave man "types and shadows" under the Old Covenant. They included animal sacrifices to lessen the severity of His judgment toward man, because man was looking forward to the cross.

An Unchanging Agreement

Certain things were secured for us when the blood of Jesus was spilled. Now those things are offered in the form of what God calls the new agreement. This agreement will not change. There will be no additions to it.

The Bible is an agreement. The Bible is alive. It's full of power. I agree to every term in the Bible. I initial what I agree with.

All along the way, I find new things in the Word of God. I say, "God, I didn't see that in there. I'm going to initial it. I'm in agreement with it."

God is neither going to add to it nor violate it. Religion has tried to make God a liar regarding His Word for too long. He is not going to lie because of man's theology. After all their theology — after all their doctrine, after all their bylaws, after all their denominational persuasions — has withered and faded away, the Word of God, which is God's new agreement, will last forever. Heaven and Earth will pass away, but God's Word will not!

Our Trustworthy Middle Man

So the intermediary Jesus became the intermediary of a new agreement. Other meanings of the words "intermediary" or "mediator" are "a go-between" or "a middle man." A middle man is one who brings parties together. For a middle man to be trustworthy from your perspective, he must look out for your best interests.

Jesus qualifies on both ends of the spectrum. Jesus looked out for His Father's best interests when He came to the Earth. He represented God fully. He didn't water down what God had to say. He didn't lie about God's will for man. When He died and rose again, He went up into heaven with His own blood to represent us fully.

When He entered into God's throne room, He didn't enter from a position of ignorance. He entered from an informed, experienced position.

He had already been tempted. He had already suffered. He had already become acquainted with everything we go through. He died like we do — but He rose again like we will! Then He ascended on high.

And when He appeared before God, He did not slight man. He did not look out for His own interests. He is not in heaven representing God. He came to Earth representing God, but He went back to heaven representing us.

The Bible calls Jesus our high priest. A high priest represents man to God. The Bible calls Jesus our advocate, lawyer, or attorney. He's up in heaven representing us. He's looking out for our best interests, because He has our interests at heart. He is a trustworthy middle man.

The Importance of Agreement

I'll let Jesus hook me up with God any day. I don't want anyone else to hook me up with God. People tell me God is unreliable, but the middle man I know tells me that all the promises of God are "yea and amen" in Him.

Why should I listen to outsiders when God's own representative has become *my* representative to God? He knows both viewpoints. He's looking out for both sides. He's bringing both parties together to make one new man.

Not only is Jesus the go-between or middle man for two parties; He is the middle man of an agreement. The Bible says, "Can two walk together, except they be *agreed?*" (Amos 3:3).

What is "an agreement"? It's like a lease or a contract. It's anything with terms that you agree to. In my dealings in the world, there have been times when I didn't read the fine print before signing an agreement. This can be a dangerous mistake.

In such cases, one party might not like the way things are going and say, "Wait a minute! What are you doing? You told me such-and-such." The other party counters, "Do you have it *in writing?*" Once it's in writing and it's signed by both parties, it's final. That's it. You either made a good deal, or you made a bad deal, but you're stuck with the deal you made.

We made a *good* deal when we allowed Jesus Christ to mediate this new agreement for us. However, the thief will not stay away just because we've been given a good deal. The thief will not stand idly by and allow us to get our percentage, our royalties, or our other benefits of the lease without a fight. The thief will act like there is no agreement. The thief will act like there is no basis for our confidence.

One of the most significant areas the devil wants to control is the area of our finances. That's why he has literally taken the message of increase and prosperity out of the pulpit. He doesn't want people to acknowledge it is in the agreement. If they did, these finances would go into the kingdom of God rather than to the ungodly.

Why Man Couldn't Negotiate

As we have seen, there is one negotiator between God and man, the man Christ Jesus. He is the mediator or negotiator of the new agreement that has been made between God and man. The *Goodspeed* translation says, "We came to Jesus, the negotiator of a new agreement."

The new agreement was a good deal. It was negotiated from a position of strength. Man didn't have any strength to negotiate under the Old Covenant, because all he had was the blood of bulls and goats. He couldn't ask God for more. He couldn't demand his rights. If he demanded his *rights,* he went directly to hell!

The new agreement was negotiated from Christ's position of victory. He could say, "Father, I shed My blood. The blood is enough payment. The payment has been made in full. I bought them back. They belong to Me. Now if they simply believe in what I did, they will have a new nature. They will become children of God. The devil has nothing in them.

"As far as the East is from the West, I have removed their transgressions from them. There is therefore now no condemnation for them. The law of the Spirit of life has made them free from the law of sin and death. There is no more need of penalty. There is no more need to make payment. They qualify for all My benefits."

As a matter of fact, Jesus said to the Father, "You know I paid the price. Father, You don't have anything more than Me to give to ransom mankind. You love them so much, You gave them heaven's best. There is nothing in heaven that can add to the sacrifice of heaven that was made. *The price was paid in full!* What Adam did, selling mankind into slavery, has been reversed completely."

Continuing in His role as our negotiator, Jesus said, "Father, they qualify for everything we have; and just as I am Your Son and heir, I have made them sons and daughters through Me."

Divine Justice Satisfied

The negotiation of the New Covenant is not happening today; Jesus is not doing this today. He did it when He walked into the holy of holies with His own blood and sprinkled it on the mercy seat.

Do you know what happened then? God the Father said, "You have successfully satisfied divine justice. I call it done. I will not hold transgressions against You. I can't hold transgressions against mankind, because the price to erase all sin was paid when My Son shed His blood. I agree to the terms of the new contract which can only be agreed upon by a divine God and a redeemed people. I agree to that contract."

At that time, there was no written contract; there was nothing on paper. We have to go to the old contract to find out what the Old Testament prophets said about the New Covenant. They said, "It's going to happen." They were looking forward to it.

Jesus said, "Now I am going to sit down, Father. I am going to send the Comforter, who is not going to speak of Himself. He is the Spirit of truth. He can't violate the agreement. The Spirit of truth will remind them what I told them. He will lead them into all truth that is in our new agreement with them — the new contract — and show them things to come." (See John 16.)

And Jesus sent the Holy Ghost. Do you know what the Holy Ghost did? He filled men and women and spoke through them. Before long, men put it down on paper, and now we have the new and better agreement.

Sign the Contract

I grew up "religious." I made up my mind after being born again that I was going to take God at His Word, so I started signing my name to what God has already signed His Name to.

There are Christians who say, "I don't need anything. I don't want anything. I don't want to be rich. It's all in the Lord's hands." They've got the contract filed away with only one signature on it!

The Father and His Son not only signed the new contract; they sent the Holy Ghost to enforce it. God the Father and His Son Jesus are the witnesses, and they have signed with one signature. There's an empty line with your name printed right next to it. Put your signature on the Word of God!

When I found out about this new agreement, I trusted the witness who mediated it, so I signed before I read the fine print. I said, "It's got to be a good deal! Let me sign, and later on I'll peruse it and find what I signed for. Where do I sign? It's a done deal!"

The First Murder on Earth

Now notice Hebrews 12:24, which we are still studying: "And to Jesus the mediator of the new covenant, and to the blood of sprinkling, that speaketh better things than that of Abel."

We came to the new agreement, and we came to Jesus, the negotiator of it. We came to the blood of sprinkling that speaks of better things than that of Abel. It is noteworthy that Abel's blood is mentioned.

Do you realize that the first murder that ever took place on planet Earth was over an offering?

The Bible says that Abel brought some of the firstlings of his flock. His brother, Cain, brought some of his vegetables. The connotation is that Cain didn't bring his firstfruits; he brought his leftovers! He didn't take the offering seriously, and he didn't put God first. He brought his offering "religiously." The Bible tells us that God had respect for Abel's offering, but He did not have respect for Cain's offering.

So Cain got mad. God knows when you get mad, and God asked Cain, "Why are you angry, and why is your countenance fallen?" (Genesis 4:6). That's an interesting term. Do you know how your countenance falls? When the smile is gone, the shout is gone, and the excitement is gone, your features fall. It's not normal for a child of God to look like this.

"Why art thou wroth? and why is thy countenance fallen? If thou doest well, shalt thou not be accepted?" God said, "And if thou doest not well, sin lieth at the door. And unto thee shall be his desire, and thou shalt rule over him" (Genesis 4:6,7).

An Explosive Conversation

Then the Bible says, "And Cain talked with Abel his brother: and it came to pass, when they were in the field, that Cain rose up against Abel his brother, and slew him" (Genesis 4:8).

Notice, Cain talked to Abel. I wonder what they talked about. This was after God had told Cain, "Why are you angry?" I think Cain probably told Abel, "Why does God respect your offering, and He doesn't respect my offering?" Abel probably told him, "Maybe it's because I put God first. You didn't put any faith in the offering, and you brought whatever was left over."

We don't want to add to the Bible, but whatever they said resulted in Cain getting hot enough to rise up and kill his brother. They really got into it, didn't they? And it was over — the offering. It was over increase. It was over prosperity! And Cain killed Abel.

So the Lord said in Genesis 4:9, "Cain, Where is Abel thy brother?" Of course, God knew. Cain replied, "I don't know. Am I my brother's keeper?" Lying thing!

Cain's Curse

And God said,

...What hast thou done? the voice of thy brother's blood crieth unto me from the ground.

And now art thou cursed from the earth, which hath opened her mouth to receive thy brother's blood from thy hand;

> **When thou tillest the ground, it shall not henceforth yield unto thee her strength; a fugitive and a vagabond shalt thou be in the earth.**
>
> **Genesis 4:10-12**

I want to show you two things from this story. The first is that *as a result of this murder, the curse of poverty entered the world!*

Anyone with half a brain can tell you if a farmer is tilling the ground and it is not yielding to him as it once did — and if he's a vagabond and a fugitive in the Earth — it must mean that the terms "curse" and "poverty" are synonymous.

Some will argue, "Poverty to me has been a blessing in disguise." If so, God should have told Cain, "From now on, you're going to grow more fruit of the ground than you can handle." *That* would have been a curse in disguise.

Poverty Is a Curse!

No, poverty is not a blessing in disguise. *Poverty is a curse, period!* And why should people who have been redeemed from the curse continue to live in it?

Someone may read this and say, "Dr. Harfouche says if you're poor, you're cursed." That's not true. How can you be a child of God and be *cursed?* I tell you, regardless of where you are financially — whether you have anything or not — you've *already* been redeemed from the curse! You might as well know you've been redeemed from it so you can benefit from what the agreement has promised you.

If we spiritualize this, we notice the issue was over an offering. Abel brought the best, the firstfruits, which the Bible tells us to bring. Cain brought an offering of his vegetables. When he saw that God had more respect for his brother's offering than his, he talked to his brother. Obviously the conversation didn't comfort Cain. He got angry and killed his brother!

Killing the Message

Often when we begin to honor God with our substance and the firstfruits of our increase, He blesses us, and the religious folks, who claim they've been giving to God and He isn't blessing them, want to talk. "I don't know why God isn't doing it for me," they say.

If you preach the truth to them or suggest, "Let's examine your life," they want to kill you. If they can't kill you, they kill the message you're carrying. Then they call you names and even say you're in a cult.

I've run into preachers who have been in the ministry 40 or 50 years but have never opened a book by Kenneth E. Hagin or Kenneth Copeland, because religion has murdered their message. These preachers won't read the truth, because the message these men preach was murdered — yet the blood of that message that was killed by religion is calling out to God.

So the devil will try to keep you from listening to or reading books by persons preaching the truth. I guarantee you there are people in Pensacola, Florida, who have never heard us, and they're scared to hear us. They've been told not to listen to us. They are manipulated by "vagabonds" who can't even get a crop.

Motivated by Fear

Sometimes people ask me, "Do you mean it's all right to read this book about faith and prosperity?" I tell them, "Oh, yes, go ahead." They read the book, and the next thing you know, they've ordered dozens of books on these subjects. They discovered that prejudices had been planted in their minds, and their decisions were based on ignorance.

Some Christians are so motivated by fear, they avoid anyplace the devil is. All someone has to do is tell the average Christian something scary, and it frightens them away. That's why we're committed to raising a generation that's not afraid of the devil.

It's time we realized that the power within us is greater than a seance. That power within us is greater than a psychic network. That power within us is greater than satanism.

It's not time to be fear-motivated; it's time to realize that if God puts His blessing on your life, you need to explore everything that is contained in the contract. You need to find out what you have signed for!

The Blood Speaks

So Cain, instead of doing well and having his offering accepted, didn't do well and didn't listen to the voice of his brother. He tried to get rid of the witness of his brother, but he couldn't, and he ended up living under the curse. The ground wouldn't cooperate with him!

That's important, because in Hebrews 12:24, God uses the blood of Abel to describe what the New Testament blessing provides, saying, "...Jesus the mediator of the new covenant, and to *the blood* of sprinkling, *that speaketh* better things than that of Abel."

We know the blood speaks. The blood of Abel cried out to God from the ground; but the blood of Jesus doesn't cry out to God from the ground, because Jesus went up into heaven with His own blood. He walked into the holy of holies with His blood. The blood of Jesus speaks to God from the throne, because Jesus sprinkled the mercy seat with it.

The blood of Jesus is not crying for vengeance. The blood of Jesus provides forgiveness and benefits.

Remember, Jesus was not a casualty! Jesus was payment in full. Jesus was not murdered. Jesus gave His life freely! His blood rose from the dead to guarantee the promises of God, based on the fact that payment for mankind's sins was made in full.

Life in the Blood

That's why the blood of Jesus is not *crying* to God from the Earth. It is *speaking* to God from the heavenlies. It's awesome!

Since Jesus is the negotiator of the New Covenant, I would venture to say that the blood of Jesus must be speaking things in line with the new agreement. Otherwise, His blood would be contradicting His negotiation. And His blood can't contradict His negotiation — because the life of the flesh is in the blood.

That means *the life Jesus lived on Earth was concentrated in His blood.* When He shed His blood, He gave His life's blood. When He gave His life's blood, He gave His life. And when He gave His life, He gave *everything!*

That life appears before God as a witness of His earthly payment for us, and it has to speak consistently with His negotiation in the contract. That's awesome, too. That gives me boldness!

Don't Refuse the Offer

The writer of Hebrews says we came to Jesus, the negotiator of a new agreement. The negotiator tells you, "Sign right here. Don't worry about it. I read the contract. Everything is in order. I got you a good deal. Sign!"

So Jesus says one thing. Then His blood — the blood of sprinkling — speaks of better things than that of Abel. We have to conclude that Jesus' blood speaks consistently with His negotiations.

Hebrews 12:25 says, "See that ye refuse not him that speaketh." How is Jesus speaking? He is speaking by His blood. He is speaking by His contract. He is speaking by the power behind the contract — the blood.

Verse 25 continues, "...For if they escaped not who refused him that spake on earth, much more shall not we escape, if we turn away from him that speaketh from heaven."

The word "refused" is derived from the Greek word *paraiteomai*. It means "decline." So this verse could read, "See that you don't decline Him who is speaking."

Jesus says, "Sign right here, son."

Don't reply, "Oh, no, I'll pass."

People who decline what Jesus offers usually blame God for their lives.

"Decline" can also mean "shun" or "ignore." Religious people ignore you — because if they don't ignore you, they'll end up killing you! The only alternative is, they have to agree with you, and that's beyond them. According to the concordance, "decline" can also mean "to avoid," "to refuse," or "to make an excuse."

The Price of Refusing

Jesus says that He is the negotiator of a new agreement between God and you, and His blood speaks better things than Abel's. See that you don't refuse Him who is speaking.

Why? If you refuse Him and don't sign your name on the new agreement, you can't claim the residuals. You can't claim the percentages. You can't claim the benefits outlined in that agreement.

You can't come back 10 years later and say, "Why didn't it work?" Jesus will say, "Show Me where you signed. Show Me where you took Me at My Word and accepted what I said. Show Me where you really put the kingdom of God first and stuck with it all your life."

If you do sign the new agreement, you can always claim your residuals. And if you don't get the benefits, you can call headquarters and ask, "Where's the check?"

Perhaps they'll say, "We sent it."

"Well, it didn't get here."

"Are you sure it's yours?"

"Oh, yes, I've got the contract right here."

"How do you know it's yours?"

"The blood is speaking, the context is speaking — and if you recall, *I signed the contract.*"

"We'll put someone right on it! We'll dispatch some angels right now, and we'll find out if the thief is breaking into your mail. We'll catch the thief, and we'll recover everything."

Then you can say, "I appreciate it. From now on, put someone on the job 24 hours a day, and make sure my money gets to me. Thank you."

Religious Addenda

An agreement is not valid unless it is signed by *both* parties. There is no place on the agreement for witnesses other than the Son of God and the Holy Ghost. You can't get Uncle Henry or Pastor Jones to sign. There is no place for them.

See that you don't make an excuse. You can't claim what's in the contract if you have an addendum to it. An addendum is signed with only one signature — yours.

We come up with religious addenda like this: "Does God heal all our diseases?" Yes, but that addendum has only one signature on it — religion's. That addendum is not valid in heaven. It doesn't qualify up there. God doesn't have a copy of it.

So don't make excuses, and don't reject the new agreement. The word "refuse" is also the word "reject." How do you reject it? Jesus comes to you and says, "I've got a deal for you." You can refuse the deal, but the Bible says, "See that you don't refuse it." Why? Because if you refuse it, you can't escape the inherent consequences.

Most people think the Bible says that you'd better keep the letter of the Law, or God will hit you in the head with a baseball bat. God doesn't need to hit you in the head with a baseball bat.

No Protection

The moment you reject the agreement, baseball bats will come at you from every direction. All you need to do is look at the world, and you'll see how badly they are beaten up. When you violate the agreement, you no longer have its divine protection.

The consequences of rejecting this blessing and agreement is to operate in the world without it. And how can you escape an ungodly, unholy, murdering tyrant like the devil if you refuse to come in agreement with God's blessings by signing on the dotted line of His new agreement?

If you don't put God in charge of your life, to include your finances and your plans, it means you're trusting in another mediator. You sign that other agreement because you think some scheme, plot, way, education, pursuit, or friend will get you better dividends than the One who has provided you the deal with heaven.

What happens is, you find you got the short end of the stick. How can you escape the fact that there is no better negotiator — no better deal securer, mediator, or go-between — than the Lord Jesus Christ. He speaks today by His Word and His blood. You should be glad you're hooked up with Jesus!

This Is the Sum

Hebrews 8:1 says, "Now of the things which we have spoken this is the sum...." In other words, this is the conclusion of what has been discussed earlier. The passage continues in verses 1-8:

...We have such an high priest, who is set on the right hand of the throne of the Majesty in the heavens;

A minister of the sanctuary, and of the true tabernacle, which the Lord pitched, and not man.

This refers to the permanent tabernacle, not the temporary tabernacle.

For every high priest is ordained to offer gifts and sacrifices....

Every high priest is ordained to offer gifts and sacrifices on behalf of the people.

...wherefore it is of necessity that this man have somewhat also to offer.

For Jesus to qualify to be a high priest, He must have something to offer, and He must offer it on behalf of the people. A high priest represents the people to God.

For if he were on earth, he should not be a priest, seeing that there are priests that offer gifts according to the law.

Why? Because Jesus' sacrifice was different from the ones that were offered for the Law. The priests of the Law offered a goat, a bullock, a sheep, or a turtledove.

A High Priest of the New Testament

Jesus offered Himself! If He was to be a high priest of the Law, He wouldn't qualify. He had to be a high priest of the New Testament. He had to be a high priest that operates not on Earth but in heaven to qualify for what we are about to discuss.

...seeing that there are priests that offer gifts according to the law:

Who serve unto the example and shadow of heavenly things, as Moses was admonished of God when he was about to make the tabernacle: for, See, saith he, that thou make all things according to the pattern shewed to thee in the mount.

God wanted the sacrifice done exactly as He stated so it would be a right type, a right shadow, a prototype, a good preview, and a lesson to prepare you for the better covenant that was to come after the Law.

But now hath he ordained a more excellent ministry, by how much also he is the mediator of a better covenant, which was established upon better promises.

Jesus obtained a more excellent ministry than earthly high priests. How? The Bible says He was the mediator, negotiator, go-between, or intercessor of a better contract between God and man. Therefore, Jesus' ministry does more for us than anything the ministry of Old Testament high priests could ever provide, which was merely a temporary *covering* of sin, not eternal redemption.

As you can see from their history, the people of Israel went about their lives and prospered as a result of the high priest's annual offering on their behalf.

Now we get into the New Testament. Verse 6 says that Jesus' ministry is a more excellent ministry. How much more excellent? God said it is as excellent as the deal He negotiated between God and man; the deal that was established on better promises.

Members of the Church — the Body of Christ — ought to be the most blessed, the healthiest, the happiest, the strongest, and the most prosperous people on planet Earth. And we will be, for we are coming to that place. We are wiping the dark ages away from us!

Eternal Redemption

Now let's read Hebrews 9:11-13:

But Christ being come an high priest of good things to come, by a greater and more perfect tabernacle, not made with hands, that is to say, not of this building;

Neither by the blood of goats and calves, but by his own blood he entered in once into the holy place, having obtained eternal redemption for us.

For if the blood of bulls and of goats, and the ashes of an heifer sprinkling the unclean, sanctifieth to the purifying of the flesh.

Under the Old Covenant, the blood of sacrificial animals worked. When the Jewish people looked forward to the true sacrifice (Jesus) through the power of faith, the animal sacrifices temporarily sanctified and purified their flesh.

How much more do you think the blood of Jesus will do for you? How much more will it do for you than turtledove blood? How much more will it do for you than goat or bull blood?

How much more shall the blood of Christ, who through the eternal Spirit offered himself without spot to God, purge your conscience from dead works to serve the living God?

And for this cause he is the mediator of the new testament, that by means of death, for the redemption of the transgressions that were under the first testament, they which are called might receive the promise of eternal inheritance.

Hebrews 9:14,15

Eternal Inheritance

Notice, for this cause Jesus is the mediator, the go-between, or the negotiator of the New Testament or the new agreement. Why? So that through His death He could redeem our transgressions, and we would receive the promise of eternal inheritance.

The moment you read "eternal inheritance," you think "eternal life." That's the only inheritance you think about. That's what religion has brainwashed you to think.

It's almost as if we've divorced God from His giving nature that operated in the Old Covenant for the Jews through the blood of bulls and goats. Some Christians assume the blood of Christ only provides a spiritual experience and an eternal security.

But when this verse refers to an eternal inheritance, it's referring to your becoming an heir. An inheritance is what you get when you're included in a will. A will is normally the distribution of an estate, or everything owned by the person who made the will.

This is the will and testament of the Lord Jesus Christ. When Jesus gave us His will, He gave these great and exceedingly precious promises to us so we, through His blood, can step into becoming partakers of an eternal inheritance.

What does God own? *Everything!* The Earth is the Lord's and the fullness thereof. He owns the cattle on a thousand hills. "The silver is mine, the gold is mine, and I will fill this house with glory, says the Lord of hosts."

An eternal inheritance, the Bible says. What are you going to inherit? You're going to inherit in this life what God has supplied for this life. And you're going to inherit in the next life what God has supplied for the next life.

Whatever is mine today, I will sign on the dotted line and receive. If the stripes on Jesus' back paid for my healing, I'm not going to wait to die to be healed; I'm going to sign on the dotted line and claim my healing right now! That's how excellent Jesus' ministry is.

The word "mediator" also means "intercessor." Hebrews 7:25 says Jesus ever lives to make intercession for us. So Jesus is not only a negotiator and a go-between in that negotiation; He also intercedes and completes individual transactions based on that extensive contract.

Jesus' Excellent Ministry

When you are standing on the promises, the Bible says Jesus' ministry is an excellent one. Why? Because He's not down here on Earth; He's up there in heaven.

His ministry is as excellent as the promises the covenant is built upon. His ministry is as excellent as the accomplishments the blood has fulfilled. It is as excellent as the Word tells us. It is excellent enough to make you an heir or an inheritor of everything that God has put in the contract for you.

Christ is the agent through whom God channels and floods your life to fulfill the contract for you. If you allow Him to have His way, you are hooked up to a ministry of excellence.

He will never fail to cause the ground to yield for you, to cause goodness and mercy to follow you, to cause your needs to be met, or to cause your finances to be supplied.

Confession

I see the contract. I'm not even going to wait to know it. I'm going to sign now on the dotted line.

I see the signature of the Father; I see the signature of the Son; and I have the help of the Holy Ghost. I sign this with my faith. I come in agreement with it, and I vow to uphold the contract as the truth in my life.

I will never file it away or doubt its content. I will contend for every syllable, every sentence, and every phrase in this agreement. Thank You, Jesus, for my inheritance!

Other books by Dr. Christian and Pastor Robin Harfouche

Dr. Christian Harfouche
Authority Over Powers of Darkness
Crossing From Death to Life
Doing the Impossible
The Hidden Power of Your Words
How To Receive Your Miracle
Living on the Cutting Edge
The Miracle Ministry of the Prophet
Personal Power in This Present Life
The Spirit Guide

Robin Harfouche
A Channel of Deceit

For more information contact:

Global Revival Distribution
4317 N. Palafox St.
Pensacola, FL. 32505
1-850-439-9750

www.globalrevival.com